_____

to

_____

from

_____

date

How's your relationship
with Jesus?

GOD'S
PROMISES®
for the
AMERICAN
PATRIOT

Dr. Richard G. Lee | Jack Countryman

NASHVILLE   DALLAS   MEXICO CITY   RIO DE JANEIRO

Published in Nashville, Tennessee, by Thomas Nelson®.

Cover design: Belinda Bass
Interior design: Kristy L. Edwards
Managing Editor: Lisa Stilwell

Thomas Nelson titles may be purchased in bulk for educational, business, fund-raising, or sales promotional use. For information, please e-mail SpecialMarkets@ ThomasNelson.com.

ISBN-13: 978-1-4041-9011-5 (HC)
ISBN-13: 978-0-529-10224-9 (CU)

Printed in the United States of America

13 14 15 16 17 RRD 5 4 3 2 1

www.thomasnelson.com

Table of Contents

Introduction

I t is the dream of every person to discover in his lifetime that special secret map that will guide him to hidden treasure. I believe that the book you hold in your hand is such a guide. Much of America's rich story is told in these pages, along with many wonderful promises from God's Word that have served as the very foundations upon which our nation was formed.

President Ronald Reagan said, "Inside the Bible's pages lie the answers to all the problems mankind has ever known. I hope Americans will read and study the Bible." God's Word and America's story are inseparable.

I hope that as you read, you will enjoy these stories of America's patriots and God's wonderful promises to us all. May God bless you, and may God bless America!

Dr. Richard G. Lee

T hroughout the history of our country, men and women have looked to God's Word for wisdom, strength, and encouragement. Through His Word, He has guided them as they acknowledged His omnipotence. God's promises come alive when combined with the historical journey of the men and women who formed the foundation of our country. Their dependence on God and His Word has become the brick and mortar for our Christian heritage. Each passage of Scripture has been chosen to help the reader appreciate our history and God's promises.

Jack Countryman

"Thanksgiving Proclamation"

City of New York, October 3, 1789

Whereas it is the duty of all Nations to acknowledge the providence of Almighty God, to obey his will, to be grateful for his benefits, and humbly to implore his protection and favor, and Whereas both Houses of Congress have by their joint Committee requested me "to recommend to the People of the United States a day of public thanksgiving and prayer to be observed by acknowledging with grateful hearts the many signal favors of Almighty God, especially by affording them an opportunity peaceably to establish a form of government for their safety and happiness."

Now therefore I do recommend and assign Thursday the 26th. day of November next to be devoted by the People of these States to the service of that great and glorious Being, who is the beneficent Author of all the good that was, that is, or that will be. That we may then all unite in rendering unto him our sincere and humble thanks, for his kind care and protection of the People of this country previous to their becoming a Nation, for the signal and manifold mercies, and the favorable interpositions of his providence, which we experienced in the course and conclusion of the late war, for the great degree of tranquility, union, and plenty, which we have since enjoyed,

2

for the peaceable and rational manner in which we have been enabled to establish constitutions of government for our safety and happiness, and particularly the national One now lately instituted, for the civil and religious liberty with which we are blessed, and the means we have of acquiring and diffusing useful knowledge and in general for all the great and various favors which he hath been pleased to confer upon us.

And also that we may then unite in most humbly offering our prayers and supplications to the great Lord and Ruler of Nations and beseech him to pardon our national and other transgressions, to enable us all, whether in public or private stations, to perform our several and relative duties properly and punctually, to render our national government a blessing to all the People, by constantly being a government of wise, just and constitutional laws, discreetly and faithfully executed and obeyed, to protect and guide all Sovereigns and Nations (especially such as have shown kindness unto us) and to bless them with good government, peace, and concord. To promote the knowledge and practice of true religion and virtue, and the encrease of science among them and Us, and generally to grant unto all Mankind such a degree of temporal prosperity as he alone knows to be best.

G. Washington

www.libraryofcongress.com

From our nation's earliest days, God's promise in 2 Chronicles 7 that He will hear the cry of a humbled people has motivated America's leaders to call citizens to prayer. In 1775, as it began the process of forming a new nation, the Continental Congress called for a day of prayer. At critical junctures during the Civil War, President Abraham Lincoln called for the nation to fast and pray. And in 1952, President Truman signed a bill establishing an annual National Day of Prayer.

Second Chronicles helps establish a model of national spiritual renewal. The book recounts how a succession of righteous kings in Judah led to reforms that brought the people back to true faith in God. Second Chronicles 16:9 assures us that God will "show Himself strong" toward those who place their trust in Him.

If My people who are called by My name will humble themselves, and pray and seek My face, and turn from their wicked ways, then I will hear from heaven, and will forgive their sin and heal their land.

2 CHRONICLES 7:14

* * * *

If we confess our sins, He is faithful and just to forgive us our sins and to cleanse us from all unrighteousness.

1 JOHN 1:9

* * * *

Call to Me, and I will answer you, and show you great and mighty things, which you do not know.

JEREMIAH 33:3

* * * *

Save now, I pray, O LORD;
    O LORD, I pray, send now prosperity.

PSALM 118:25

A dopted on July 4, 1776, the Declaration of Independence stated that the thirteen American colonies were "Free and Independent States" and that "all political connection between them and the State of Great Britain, is and ought to be totally dissolved." Our Founding Fathers acknowledged God as the source of our rights:

> We hold these truths to be self-evident, that all men are created equal, that they are endowed by their Creator with certain unalienable Rights, that among these are Life, Liberty and the pursuit of Happiness—That to secure these rights, Governments are instituted among Men, deriving their just Powers from the consent of the governed—That whenever any Form of Government becomes destructive of these ends, it is the Right of the People to alter or to abolish it, and to institute new Government, laying its foundation on such principles and organizing its powers in such form, as to them shall seem most likely to effect their Safety and Happiness....
>
> For the support of this Declaration, with a firm reliance on the protection of Divine Providence, we mutually pledge to each other our Lives, our Fortunes and our sacred Honor.

As Founding Father Benjamin Rush said:
> Without [religion] there can be no virtue, and without virtue there can be no liberty, and liberty is the object and life of all republican governments.

6

There is therefore now no condemnation to those who are in Christ Jesus, who do not walk according to the flesh, but according to the Spirit. For the law of the Spirit of life in Christ Jesus has made me free from the law of sin and death.

ROMANS 8:1–2

* * * *

Happy is he who has the God of Jacob for his help,
　　Whose hope is in the LORD his God,
Who made heaven and earth,
　　The sea, and all that is in them;
　　Who keeps truth forever,
Who executes justice for the oppressed,
　　Who gives food to the hungry.
　　The LORD gives freedom to the prisoners.

PSALM 146:5–7

* * * *

Now the Lord is the Spirit; and where the Spirit of the Lord is, there is liberty.

2 CORINTHIANS 3:17

Noah Webster's *An American Dictionary of the English Language*, 1828:

> *patriotism*, n. Love of one's country; the passion which aims to serve one's country, either in defending it from invasion, or protecting its rights and maintaining its laws and institutions in vigor and purity. Patriotism is the characteristic of a good citizen, the noblest passion that animates a man in the character of a citizen.

Merriam-Webster's Collegiate Dictionary, Eleventh Edition, copyright © 2004:

> *patriotism*, n. Love for or devotion to one's country.

Note how the definitions have changed. With its objective actions, Noah Webster's patriotism is very different from the vague, subjective patriotism of one who only feels love for his country. True patriotism is not just an emotional feeling; it is action.

Webster's original definition starts with a love for country but moves to specific actions: service to country, defense of country, protection of the rights of country, maintenance of the laws and institutions of country, and preservation of religion and morality in public and private life. This kind of patriotism puts the needs of the country above personal or partisan desires, as well as above the favor of foreign nations.

And the LORD commanded us to observe all these
statutes, to fear the LORD our God, for our good always,
that He might preserve us alive, as it is this day.

DEUTERONOMY 6:24

＊ ＊ ＊ ＊

Let your heart therefore be loyal to the LORD our God,
to walk in His statutes and keep His commandments, as
at this day.

1 KINGS 8:61

＊ ＊ ＊ ＊

So every man of Israel . . . remained loyal to their king.

2 SAMUEL 20:2

＊ ＊ ＊ ＊

Let every soul be subject to the governing authorities.
For there is no authority except from God, and the
authorities that exist are appointed by God. . . .

Render therefore to all their due: taxes to whom taxes
are due . . . fear to whom fear, honor to whom honor.

ROMANS 13:1, 7

Hear the confident declaration of American statesman Daniel Webster (1782–1852):

The Gospel is either true history, or it is a consummate fraud; it is either a reality or an imposition. Christ was what He professed to be, or He was an imposter. There is no other alternative. His spotless life in His earnest enforcement of the truth—His suffering in its defense, forbid us to suppose that He was suffering an illusion of a heated brain. Every act of His pure and holy life shows that He was the author of truth, the advocate of truth, the earnest defender of truth, and the uncompromising sufferer for truth. Now, considering the purity of His doctrines, the simplicity of His life, and the sublimity of His death, is it possible that He would have died for an illusion? In all His preaching the Savior made no popular appeals. His discourses were always directed to the individual. Christ and His apostles sought to impress upon every man the conviction that he must stand or fall alone—he must live for himself, and die for himself, and give up his account to the omniscient God as though he were the only dependent creature in the universe. The Gospel leaves the individual sinner alone with himself and his God.

Daniel Webster

10

For unto us a Child is born, unto us a Son is given;
And the government will be upon His shoulder.
And His name will be called
Wonderful, Counselor, Mighty God,
Everlasting Father, Prince of Peace.

ISAIAH 9:6

★ ★ ★ ★

Now when all things are made subject to Him, then the
Son Himself will also be subject to Him who put all
things under Him, that God may be all in all.

1 CORINTHIANS 15:28

★ ★ ★ ★

Jesus said to him, "I am the way, the truth, and the life.
No one comes to the Father except through Me."

JOHN 14:6

E lias Boudinot Jr. (1740–1821) was an American
lawyer and statesman from Elizabeth, New Jersey.
An energetic patriot, he was elected a delegate to the
Continental Congress from 1777–1784, serving as its
president from 1782–1783. He then served three terms
in Congress and ten years as Director of the Mint.
Boudinot supported many civic and educational causes
during his life, including serving as one of Princeton's
trustees for nearly half a century.

Boudinot was elected president of the American
Bible Society at its founding in 1816. In accepting the
office, he wrote that this was "the greatest honor" that
could have been conferred upon him "this side of the
grave." He had an unwavering faith that God had called
the men of the society to the work of making Bibles
available in America. His ten-thousand-dollar gift, at a
time when an annual salary of four hundred
dollars was considered good, essentially
enabled the formation and organization
of the American Bible Society, which
still sponsors the work of Bible
translation and distribution around
the world.

Elias Boudinot Jr.

Therefore gird up the loins of your mind, be sober, and rest your hope fully upon the grace that is to be brought to you at the revelation of Jesus Christ; as obedient children, not conforming yourselves to the former lusts, as in your ignorance; but as He who called you is holy, you also be holy in all your conduct, because it is written, "Be holy, for I am holy."

1 Peter 1:13–16

* * * *

Therefore the Lord God of Israel says: "I said indeed that your house and the house of your father would walk before Me forever." But now the Lord says: "Far be it from Me; for those who honor Me I will honor, and those who despise Me shall be lightly esteemed."

1 Samuel 2:30

* * * *

Do not be deceived, God is not mocked; for whatever a man sows, that he will also reap. For he who sows to his flesh will of the flesh reap corruption, but he who sows to the Spirit will of the Spirit reap everlasting life.

Galatians 6:7–8

A gricultural chemist George Washington Carver (1864–1943) discovered three hundred uses for peanuts and hundreds more uses for soybeans, pecans, and sweet potatoes. Read his thoughts about God:

As a very small boy exploring the almost virgin woods of the old Carver place, I had the impression someone had just been there ahead of me. Things were so orderly, so clean, so harmoniously beautiful. A few years later in this same woods . . . I was practically overwhelmed with the sense of some Great Presence. Not only had someone been there. Someone was there. . . .

Years later when I read in the Scriptures, "In Him we live and move and have our being," I knew what the writer meant. Never since have I been without this consciousness of the Creator speaking to me. . . . The out-of-doors has been to me more and more a great cathedral in which God could be continuously spoken to and heard from. . . .

Man, who needed a purpose, a mission, to keep him alive, had one. He could be . . . God's co-worker. . . . My purpose alone must be God's purpose—to increase the welfare and happiness of His people. . . . Why, then, should we who believe in Christ be so surprised at what God can do with a willing man in a laboratory?

George Washington Carver in his laboratory

14

Serve the LORD with gladness;
   Come before His presence with singing.
Know that the LORD, He is God;
   It is He who has made us, and not we ourselves;
   We are His people and the sheep of His pasture.

PSALM 100:2–3

★ ★ ★ ★

"If anyone serves Me, let him follow Me; and where I am, there My servant will be also. If anyone serves Me, him My Father will honor."

JOHN 12:26

★ ★ ★ ★

Let love be without hypocrisy. Abhor what is evil. Cling to what is good. Be kindly affectionate to one another with brotherly love, in honor giving preference to one another; not lagging in diligence, fervent in spirit, serving the Lord; rejoicing in hope, patient in tribulation, continuing steadfastly in prayer; distributing to the needs of the saints, given to hospitality.

ROMANS 12:9–13

As Franklin D. Roosevelt's 1939 State of the Union underscores, until recent years America's leaders understood the vital connection between religion and democracy. With Hitler on the move in Europe, President Roosevelt said this:

Storms from abroad directly challenge three institutions indispensable to Americans, now as always. The first is religion. It is the source of the other two—democracy and international good faith.

Religion, by teaching man his relationship to God, gives the individual a sense of his own dignity and teaches him to respect himself by respecting his neighbors.

Democracy, the practice of self-government, is a covenant among free men to respect the rights and liberties of their fellows.

International good faith, a sister of democracy, springs from the will of civilized nations of men to respect the rights and liberties of other nations of men....

There comes a time in the affairs of men when they must prepare to defend, not their homes alone, but the tenets of faith and humanity on which their churches, their governments, and their very civilization are founded. The defense of religion, of democracy, and of good faith among nations is all the same fight. To save one we must now make up our minds to save all.

Franklin D. Roosevelt

16

For the LORD your God is He who goes with you, to fight for you against your enemies, to save you.

DEUTERONOMY 20:4

* * * *

"Watch therefore, and pray always that you may be counted worthy to escape all these things that will come to pass, and to stand before the Son of Man."

LUKE 21:36

* * * *

Therefore be imitators of God as dear children. And walk in love, as Christ also has loved us and given Himself for us, an offering and a sacrifice to God for a sweet-smelling aroma. . . .

For you were once darkness, but now you are light in the Lord. Walk as children of light.

EPHESIANS 5:1–2, 8

* * * *

Finally, my brethren, be strong in the Lord and in the power of His might. Put on the whole armor of God, that you may be able to stand against the wiles of the devil.

EPHESIANS 6:10–11

L ike Ruth of the Old Testament, women of steadfast
loyalty and faith have been key to America's
strength. One such woman was Ruth Bell Graham, wife
of America's beloved twentieth-century spiritual leader
Dr. Billy Graham. Throughout their life together, Dr.
Graham often emphasized how vital his wife was to his
own success, noting that "my work through the years
would have been impossible without her encouragement
and support."

For her own part, Mrs. Graham's quiet commitment
to her God and to her family reflected the determination
of her biblical namesake to follow the God of Israel.
Mrs. Graham once explained, "I must faithfully,
patiently, lovingly, and happily do my part—then
quietly wait for God to do His." That same faithfulness
was what led the widowed and desolate Ruth of the
Bible to become the wife of Boaz and a member
of the line of Jesus Christ.

Ruth Bell Graham

18

All the ways of a man are pure in his own eyes,
But the LORD weighs the spirits.
Commit your works to the LORD,
And your thoughts will be established.

PROVERBS 16:2–3

* * * *

Therefore know that the LORD your God, He is God,
the faithful God who keeps covenant and mercy for a
thousand generations with those who love Him and
keep His commandments.

DEUTERONOMY 7:9

* * * *

Servants, be submissive to your masters with all fear, not
only to the good and gentle, but also to the harsh. For
this is commendable, if because of conscience toward
God one endures grief, suffering wrongfully.

1 PETER 2:18–19

Founding Father and one of the three authors of the Federalist Papers, Alexander Hamilton (January 11, 1755–July 12, 1804), wrote this concerning the nature of liberty:

> The fundamental source of all your errors, sophisms, and false reasonings is a total ignorance of the natural rights of mankind. Were you once to become acquainted with these, you could never entertain a thought that all men are not, by nature, entitled to a parity of privileges. You would be convinced that natural liberty is a gift of the beneficent Creator to the whole human race; and that civil liberty is founded in that and cannot be wrested from any people, without the most manifest violation of justice.

Alexander Hamilton

20

And because you are sons, God has sent forth the Spirit
of His Son into your hearts, crying out, "Abba, Father!"
Therefore you are no longer a slave but a son, and if a
son, then an heir of God through Christ.

GALATIANS 4:6–7

* * * *

"The Spirit of the LORD is upon Me,
Because He has anointed Me
To preach the gospel to the poor;
He has sent Me to heal the brokenhearted,
To proclaim liberty to the captives
And recovery of sight to the blind,
To set at liberty those who are oppressed."

LUKE 4:18

* * * *

For you, brethren, have been called to liberty; only
do not use liberty as an opportunity for the flesh, but
through love serve one another. For all the law is fulfilled
in one word, even in this: "You shall love your neighbor
as yourself."

GALATIANS 5:13–14

The apostle Paul's letter to believers in Philippi is a note of thanks for their help during his time of need. He also lovingly urged the members of the church there to center their actions and thoughts on the pursuit of the Person and power of Christ. Paul's central point was simple: only in Christ are real unity and genuine joy possible. With Christ as our model of humility and service, we believers can enjoy a oneness of purpose, attitude, goal, and labor. Paul then reminded the Philippians that their ultimate citizenship is in heaven.

However, the words of Adlai Stevenson (1900–1965), who served as the U.S. ambassador to the United Nations from 1961–1965, remind us of the privilege of being an American citizen:

> When an American says that he loves his country, he means not only that he loves the New England hills, the prairies glistening in the sun, the wide and rising plains, the great mountains, and the sea. He means that he loves an inner air, an inner light in which freedom lives and in which a man can draw the breath of self-respect.

Yet indeed I also count all things loss for the excellence of the knowledge of Christ Jesus my Lord, for whom I have suffered the loss of all things, and count them as rubbish, that I may gain Christ and be found in Him, not having my own righteousness, which is from the law, but that which is through faith in Christ, the righteousness which is from God by faith; that I may know Him and the power of His resurrection, and the fellowship of His sufferings, being conformed to His death.

PHILIPPIANS 3:8–10

★ ★ ★ ★

Brethren, I do not count myself to have apprehended; but one thing I do, forgetting those things which are behind and reaching forward to those things which are ahead, I press toward the goal for the prize of the upward call of God in Christ Jesus.

PHILIPPIANS 3:13–14

★ ★ ★ ★

For the LORD God is a sun and shield;
    The LORD will give grace and glory;
    No good thing will He withhold
    From those who walk uprightly.

PSALM 84:11

Speak Up!

As a young pastor, Titus faced the difficult assignment of setting in order the church at Crete. Paul advised him to appoint elders, men of proven spiritual character in their homes and businesses, to do the work of the church. In addition, Paul discussed in his letter to Titus that men and women, young and old, all have vital functions to fulfill in the church if they are to be living examples of the doctrine they profess.

Consider the wisdom of this statement attributed to Dr. Martin Luther King Jr., the great civil rights leader of the twentieth century: "Our lives begin to end the day we become silent about things that matter." If King did not say it, he certainly lived it. Likewise, Paul told Titus that he could not be silent about the greatest matter in human history: "the grace of God that brings salvation has appeared to all men" (2:11). Paul charged Titus to "speak these things, exhort, and rebuke with all authority" (2:15).

But as for you, speak the things which are proper for sound doctrine: that the older men be sober, reverent, temperate, sound in faith, in love, in patience; the older women likewise, that they be reverent in behavior, not slanderers, not given to much wine, teachers of good things—that they admonish the young women to love their husbands, to love their children, to be discreet, chaste, homemakers, good, obedient to their own husbands, that the word of God may not be blasphemed. Likewise, exhort the young men to be sober-minded, in all things showing yourself to be a pattern of good works; in doctrine showing integrity, reverence, incorruptibility.

TITUS 2:1–7

* * * *

Let no one despise your youth, but be an example to the believers in word, in conduct, in love, in spirit, in faith, in purity. Till I come, give attention to reading, to exhortation, to doctrine. Do not neglect the gift that is in you, which was given to you by prophecy with the laying on of the hands of the eldership. Meditate on these things; give yourself entirely to them, that your progress may be evident to all.

1 TIMOTHY 4:12–15

The civil rights movement of the 1950s and 1960s was led primarily by Dr. Martin Luther King Jr., who had become pastor of Dexter Avenue Baptist Church in Montgomery, Alabama, in 1954. At that time, American society was characterized by inequality, oppression, and segregation of black citizens, fueled by hatred, prejudice, and hostility. Refusing to stoop to such hatred and succumb to any bitterness, Dr. King connected his deep love for God and for his fellow man with the powerful determination to gain equal civil rights for African-Americans.

Dr. King rose to national prominence as the leader of the movement through nonviolent mass demonstrations. The first was the Montgomery, Alabama, bus boycott in 1956, which started after Rosa Parks was arrested for refusing to give her seat on a bus to a white man. The movement produced scores of men and women who risked, and some who gave, their lives to secure a more just and inclusive society.

Martin Luther King, Jr.

Now the Lord is the Spirit; and where the Spirit of the Lord is, there is liberty.

2 CORINTHIANS 3:17

★ ★ ★ ★

"'And you shall love the LORD your God with all your heart, with all your soul, with all your mind, and with all your strength.' This is the first commandment. And the second, like it, is this: 'You shall love your neighbor as yourself.' There is no other commandment greater than these."

MARK 12:30–31

★ ★ ★ ★

"He who is faithful in what is least is faithful also in much; and he who is unjust in what is least is unjust also in much. Therefore if you have not been faithful in the unrighteous mammon, who will commit to your trust the true riches? And if you have not been faithful in what is another man's, who will give you what is your own? 'No servant can serve two masters; for either he will hate the one and love the other, or else he will be loyal to the one and despise the other. You cannot serve God and mammon.'"

LUKE 16:10–13

In his January 20, 1989, inaugural address, George H. W. Bush said this:

We meet on democracy's front porch, a good place to talk as neighbors and as friends. For this is a day when our nation is made whole, when our differences, for a moment, are suspended.

And my first act as President is a prayer. I ask you to bow your heads:

Heavenly Father, we bow our heads and thank You for Your love. Accept our thanks for the peace that yields this day and the shared faith that makes its continuance likely. Make us strong to do Your work, willing to heed and hear Your will, and write on our hearts these words: "Use power to help people." For we are given power not to advance our own purposes, nor to make a great show in the world, nor a name. There is but one just use of power, and it is to serve people. Help us to remember it, Lord. Amen.

President George H. W. Bush

28

"Yet it shall not be so among you; but whoever desires to become great among you shall be your servant."

MARK 10:43

★ ★ ★ ★

"And the King will answer and say to them, 'Assuredly, I say to you, inasmuch as you did it to one of the least of these My brethren, you did it to Me.'"

MATTHEW 25:40

★ ★ ★ ★

And He sat down, called the twelve, and said to them, "If anyone desires to be first, he shall be last of all and servant of all."

MARK 9:35

★ ★ ★ ★

"He who loves his life will lose it, and he who hates his life in this world will keep it for eternal life. If anyone serves Me, let him follow Me; and where I am, there My servant will be also. If anyone serves Me, him My Father will honor."

JOHN 12:25–26

Henry Wadsworth Longfellow (1807–1882) was one of the the most widely known American poets in his day. Reflecting his fervent abolitionist convictions, "The Building of a Ship" speaks of his fear that the slavery issue would destroy the nation.

Thou, too, sail on, O Ship of State!
Sail on, O Union, strong and great!
Humanity with all its fears,
With all the hopes of future years,
Is hanging breathless on thy fate! …
Our hearts, our hopes, are all with thee,
Our hearts, our hopes, our prayers, our tears,
Our faith triumphant o'er our fears,
Are all with thee, —are all with thee!

In January 1941, President Franklin D. Roosevelt included the first five lines of Longfellow's poem in a handwritten letter to English Prime Minister Winston Churchill and said the verse "applies to you people as it does to us." Deeply moved, Churchill saw the letter as a symbol of the two countries' growing partnership. "Give us the tools," he told the president, "and we will finish the job!"

Henry Wadsworth Longfellow

The LORD brings the counsel of the nations to nothing;
   He makes the plans of the peoples of no effect.
The counsel of the LORD stands forever,
   The plans of His heart to all generations.
Blessed is the nation whose God is the LORD,
   The people He has chosen as His own inheritance.

PSALM 33:10–12

★ ★ ★ ★

For to this end I also wrote, that I might put you to the test, whether you are obedient in all things. Now whom you forgive anything, I also forgive. For if indeed I have forgiven anything, I have forgiven that one for your sakes in the presence of Christ.

2 CORINTHIANS 2:9–10

★ ★ ★ ★

There is no wisdom or understanding
   Or counsel against the LORD.
The horse is prepared for the day of battle,
   But deliverance is of the LORD.

PROVERBS 21:30–31

O n January 25, 1974, Ronald Reagan gave his famous "Shining City Upon a Hill" speech and concluded by saying this:

> We cannot escape our destiny, nor should we try to do so. The leadership of the free world was thrust upon us two centuries ago in that little hall of Philadelphia. In the days following World War II, when the economic strength and power of America was all that stood between the world and the return to the dark ages, Pope Pius XII said, "The American people have a great genius for splendid and unselfish actions. Into the hands of America God has placed the destinies of an afflicted mankind."

We were indeed—and we are today—the last best hope of man on earth.

President Ronald Reagan

Through whom also we have access by faith into this grace in which we stand, and rejoice in hope of the glory of God. . . . Now hope does not disappoint, because the love of God has been poured out in our hearts by the Holy Spirit who was given to us.

ROMANS 5:2, 5

For we were saved in this hope, but hope that is seen is not hope; for why does one still hope for what he sees? But if we hope for what we do not see, we eagerly wait for it with perseverance.

ROMANS 8:24–25

There is one body and one Spirit, just as you were called in one hope of your calling; one Lord, one faith, one baptism; one God and Father of all, who is above all, and through all, and in you all.

EPHESIANS 4:4–6

President Harry S. Truman held office during the end of World War II. In this 1946 speech, he reminded Americans of what we fought for and how to preserve it:

> We have just come through a decade in which forces of evil in various parts of the world have been lined up in a bitter fight to banish from the face of the earth ... religion and democracy. For these forces of evil have long realized that both religion and democracy are founded on one basic principle, the worth and dignity of the individual man and woman. Dictatorship, on the other hand, has always rejected that principle. Dictatorship, by whatever name, is founded on the doctrine that the individual amounts to nothing; that the State is the only thing that counts; and that men and women and children were put on earth solely for the purpose of serving the State....
>
> If men and nations would but live by the precepts of the ancient prophets and the teachings of the Sermon on the Mount, problems which now seem so difficult would soon disappear....
> This is a supreme opportunity for the Church to continue to fulfill its mission on earth.... Oh, for an Isaiah or a Saint Paul to reawaken this sick world to its moral responsibilities!

President Harry Truman

"But seek first the kingdom of God and His righteousness, and all these things shall be added to you."

Matthew 6:33

★ ★ ★ ★

The way of the just is uprightness;
    O Most Upright,
    You weigh the path of the just.
Yes, in the way of Your judgments,
    O Lord, we have waited for You;
    The desire of our soul is for Your name
    And for the remembrance of You.

Isaiah 26:7–8

★ ★ ★ ★

Delight yourself also in the Lord,
    And He shall give you the desires of your heart.
Commit your way to the Lord,
    Trust also in Him,
    And He shall bring it to pass.
He shall bring forth your righteousness as the light,
    And your justice as the noonday.

Psalm 37:4–6

While there have been revisions to state constitutions over the years, forty-three states acknowledge God or a higher power in their preambles, and the other seven states acknowledge God in their religious freedom provisions.

The following is a short sample from various state constitutions:

Connecticut's 1818 Preamble: "The People of Connecticut, acknowledging with gratitude the good Providence of God in permitting them to enjoy a free government . . ."

Maine's 1820 Preamble: "We the People of Maine . . . acknowledging with grateful hearts the goodness of the Sovereign Ruler of the Universe in affording us an opportunity . . . and imploring His aid and direction in its accomplishment . . ."

Massachusetts's 1780 Preamble: "We, therefore, the people of Massachusetts, acknowledging with grateful hearts, the goodness of the Great Legislator of the Universe, in affording us, in the course of His Providence, an opportunity . . . and devoutly imploring His direction . . ."

New York's 1846 Preamble: "We, the people of the State of New York, grateful to Almighty God for our freedom, in order to secure its blessings . . ."

The New York State Capitol

But let all those rejoice who put their trust in You;
    Let them ever shout for joy, because You defend
        them;
    Let those also who love Your name
    Be joyful in You.
For You, O LORD, will bless the righteous;
    With favor You will surround him as with a shield.

PSALM 5:11–12

★ ★ ★ ★

The LORD knows the days of the upright,
    And their inheritance shall be forever.
They shall not be ashamed in the evil time,
    And in the days of famine they shall be satisfied.

PSALM 37:18–19

★ ★ ★ ★

The LORD is righteous in all His ways,
    Gracious in all His works.
The LORD is near to all who call upon Him,
    To all who call upon Him in truth.

PSALM 145:17–18

S hortly before 1 a.m. on February 2, 1943, the American transport ship *Dorchester* was steaming through the icy North Atlantic from Newfoundland toward an American base in Greenland, carrying 902 servicemen, merchant seamen, and civilian workers, when a German torpedo struck the starboard side.

Through the pandemonium, four Army chaplains— George L. Fox, Methodist; Alexander D. Goode, Jewish; John P. Washington, Roman Catholic; and Clark V. Poling, Dutch Reformed—brought hope to the men struggling to survive, even taking off their own life vests and giving them to four frightened young men.

Then in the darkness, singing and shouting biblical encouragement, the four chaplains linked arms and grasped the railing of the ship as it slipped into the ocean. William Bednar said that, as he floated among dead comrades, "their voices . . . were the only thing that kept me going."

Of the men aboard the *Dorchester*, 672 died, including the chaplains. Their heroic conduct offered a vision of greatness that stunned America.

A Stained Glass Window Commemorating the Four Chaplains

"Greater love has no one than this, than to lay down one's life for his friends."

JOHN 15:13

* * * *

My covenant I will not break,
    Nor alter the word that has gone out of My lips.
Once I have sworn by My holiness;
    I will not lie to David:
His seed shall endure forever,
    And his throne as the sun before Me;
It shall be established forever like the moon,
    Even like the faithful witness in the sky.

PSALM 89:34–37

* * * *

"I am the good shepherd. The good shepherd gives His life for the sheep."

JOHN 10:11

The Bible and American Presidents

The first and almost the only book deserving of universal attention is the Bible. I speak as a man of the world . . . and I say to you, "Search the Scriptures."

JOHN QUINCY ADAMS, 6TH PRESIDENT

In regard for this Great Book, I have this to say, it is the best gift God has given to man. ALL THE GOOD THE SAVIOR GAVE TO THE WORLD WAS COMMUNICATED THROUGH THIS BOOK.

ABRAHAM LINCOLN, 16TH PRESIDENT

We cannot read the history of our rise and development as a nation without reckoning with the place the Bible has occupied in shaping the advances of the Republic. Where we have been the truest and most consistent in obeying its precepts, we have attained the greatest measure of contentment and prosperity.

FRANKLIN D. ROOSEVELT, 32ND PRESIDENT

The foundations of our society and our government rest so much on the teachings of the Bible that it would be difficult to support them if faith in these teachings would cease to be practically universal in our country.

CALVIN COOLIDGE, 30TH PRESIDENT

If you take out of your statutes,
your constitution, your family life
ALL THAT IS TAKEN FROM THE SACRED
BOOK, WHAT WOULD THERE BE LEFT
TO BIND SOCIETY TOGETHER?

BENJAMIN HARRISON, 23RD PRESIDENT

Inside the Bible's pages lie all the
answers to all of the problems man
has ever known. . . . The Bible can
touch our hearts, order our minds,
and refresh our souls.

RONALD REAGAN, 40TH PRESIDENT

The fundamental basis of this nation's laws was given
to Moses on the Mount. The fundamental basis of our
Bill of Rights comes from the teachings we get from
Exodus and Saint Matthew, from Isaiah and Saint
Paul. . . . If we don't have a proper fundamental moral
background, we will finally end up with a totalitarian
government which does not believe in rights for
anybody except the State!

HARRY S. TRUMAN, 33RD PRESIDENT

The Boy Scouts of America believes that no member can grow into the best kind of citizen without recognizing an obligation to God. Accordingly, youth members and adult volunteer leaders obligate themselves to do their duty to God and live in accordance with the Scout Oath and the Scout Law. But it hasn't been without its share of legal battles.

In *Welsh v. Boy Scouts of America* (1993), the U.S. Court of Appeals for the Seventh Circuit ruled that the Boy Scouts could keep the phrase *duty to God* in their oath and that, as a private organization, they have the right to exclude anyone who refuses to take the oath:

> The leadership of many in our government is a testimonial to the success of Boy Scout activities. In recent years, single-parent families, gang activity, availability of drugs and other factors have increased the dire need for support structures like the Scouts. When the government, in this instance through the courts, seeks to regulate the membership of an organization like the Boy Scouts in a way that scuttles its founding principles, we run the risk of undermining one of the seedbeds of virtue that cultivate the sorts of citizens our nation so desperately needs.

Cases in 1995 and 1998 also upheld the "duty to God" requirements.

Boy Scouts of America, 1941

So you shall serve the LORD your God, and He will bless your bread and your water. And I will take sickness away from the midst of you.

EXODUS 23:25

* * * *

The LORD our God we will serve, and His voice we will obey!

JOSHUA 24:24

* * * *

And now, Israel, what does the LORD your God require of you, but to fear the LORD your God, to walk in all His ways and to love Him, to serve the LORD your God with all your heart and with all your soul.

DEUTERONOMY 10:12

John McLean (1785–1861), a U.S. Postmaster General and justice of the U.S. Supreme Court, wrote this:

> No one can estimate or describe the salutary influence of the Bible. What would the world be without it? Compare the dark places of the earth, where the light of the Gospel has not penetrated, with those where it has been proclaimed and embraced in all its purity. Life and immortality are brought to light by the Scriptures. Aside from Revelation, darkness rests upon the world and upon the future. There is no ray of light to shine upon our pathway; there is no star of hope. We begin our speculations as to our destiny in conjecture, and they end in uncertainty. We know not that there is a God, a heaven, or a hell, or any day of general account, when the wicked and the righteous shall be judged. The Bible has shed a glorious light upon the world. It shows us that in the coming day we must answer for the deeds done in the body. It has opened us to a new and living way, so plainly marked out that no one can mistake it.

John McLean

For it is the God who commanded light to shine out of darkness, who has shone in our hearts to give the light of the knowledge of the glory of God in the face of Jesus Christ.

2 CORINTHIANS 4:6

★ ★ ★ ★

For the word of God is living and powerful, and sharper than any two-edged sword, piercing even to the division of soul and spirit, and of joints and marrow, and is a discerner of the thoughts and intents of the heart.

HEBREWS 4:12

★ ★ ★ ★

Every word of God is pure;
    He is a shield to those who put their trust in Him.

PROVERBS 30:5

★ ★ ★ ★

So then faith comes by hearing, and hearing by the word of God.

ROMANS 10:17

With Americans fearing war, President John F. Kennedy spoke these inspirational words in his 1961 inaugural address:

> The torch has been passed to a new generation of Americans, born in this century, tempered by war, disciplined by a hard and bitter peace, proud of our ancient heritage and unwilling to witness or permit the slow undoing of those human rights to which this nation has always been committed....
>
> In the long history of the world, only a few generations have been granted the role of defending freedom in its hour of maximum danger....The energy, the faith, the devotion which we bring to this endeavor will light our country and all who serve it—and the glow from that fire can truly light the world. And so, my fellow Americans: ask not what your country can do for you—ask what you can do for your country....
>
> With a good conscience our only sure reward, with history the final judge of our deeds, let us go forth to lead the land we love, asking His blessing and His help, but knowing that here on earth God's work must truly be our own.

John F. Kennedy

46

But as for me and my house, we will serve the LORD.

JOSHUA 24:15B

*　*　*　*

Delight yourself also in the LORD,
　　And He shall give you the desires of your heart.

PSALM 37:4

*　*　*　*

And you will seek Me and find Me, when you search for
Me with all your heart.

JEREMIAH 29:13

*　*　*　*

Then he said, "The God of our fathers has chosen you
that you should know His will, and see the Just One,
and hear the voice of His mouth."

ACTS 22:14

In the early church, many believers who had stepped out of Judaism into Christianity found themselves persecuted by nonbelieving Jews, prompting the writer of Hebrews to address the superiority of Christ over Judaism. Christ is superior to angels, the Aaronic priesthood, and the Law. In short, he argued, there is infinitely more to be gained by following Christ than to be lost by yielding up the Jewish traditions.

The recipients of the book of Hebrews faced persecution, even death, for their Christian confession, and it is worth noting that the marching song of the Union Army during the Civil War included the line "as Christ died to make men holy, let us die to make men free." Although that phrase was later changed to "let us live to make men free," for the soldiers who placed their lives on the line to end slavery and preserve the Union, the original wording was absolutely correct.

Seeing then that we have a great High Priest who has passed through the heavens, Jesus the Son of God, let us hold fast our confession.

HEBREWS 4:14

★ ★ ★ ★

Likewise the Spirit also helps in our weaknesses. For we do not know what we should pray for as we ought, but the Spirit Himself makes intercession for us with groanings which cannot be uttered.

Now He who searches the hearts knows what the mind of the Spirit is, because He makes intercession for the saints according to the will of God.

ROMANS 8:26–27

★ ★ ★ ★

Therefore He is also able to save to the uttermost those who come to God through Him, since He always lives to make intercession for them.

For such a High Priest was fitting for us, who is holy, harmless, undefiled, separate from sinners, and has become higher than the heavens.

HEBREWS 7:25–26

When the first settlers arrived in America, the influence of the Bible on their lives came with them. For many, their Christian faith was as much a part of who they were as their brave spirit was, and their faith impacted everything they did. This fact stands out boldly as one sees, again and again, Scripture reflected in the individual colonies' statements of the goal of their government. The Rhode Island Charter of 1683, for instance, begins this way: "We submit our person, lives, and estates unto our Lord Jesus Christ, the King of kings and Lord of lords, and to all those perfect and most absolute laws of His given us in His Holy Word."

In fact, from the first colony at Jamestown to the Pennsylvania Charter of Privileges granted to William Penn in 1701—where "all persons who . . . profess to believe in Jesus Christ, the Savior of the world, shall be capable . . . to serve this government in any capacity, both legislatively and executively"—the Bible was considered the rule of life in the colonies.

William Penn

50

★
★ ★

The counsel of the Lord stands forever,
   The plans of His heart to all generations.
Blessed is the nation whose God is the Lord,
   The people He has chosen as His own inheritance.

PSALM 33:11–12

★ ★ ★ ★

"But the Helper, the Holy Spirit, whom the Father will send in My name, He will teach you all things, and bring to your remembrance all things that I said to you."

JOHN 14:26

★ ★ ★ ★

They have forsaken the right way and gone astray, following the way of Balaam the son of Beor, who loved the wages of unrighteousness; but he was rebuked for his iniquity: a dumb donkey speaking with a man's voice restrained the madness of the prophet.

   These are wells without water, clouds carried by a tempest, for whom is reserved the blackness of darkness forever.

2 PETER 2:15–17

A close friend of Abe Lincoln, Joshua Speed published *Reminiscences of Abraham Lincoln*, which includes a story from 1864 when he visited Lincoln:

> When I knew [Mr. Lincoln], in early life, he was a skeptic. He had tried hard to be a believer, but his reason could not grasp and solve the great problem of redemption as taught. He was very cautious never to give expression to any thought or sentiment that would grate harshly upon a Christian's ear. For a sincere Christian, he had great respect. . . . But this was a subject we never discussed.
>
> The only evidence I have of any change, was in the summer before he was killed. I was invited out to the Soldier's Home to spend the night. As I entered the room, near night, he was sitting near a window intently reading his Bible.
>
> Approaching him I said, "I am glad to see you so profitably engaged."
>
> "Yes," said he, "I am profitably engaged."
>
> "Well," said I, "if you have recovered from your skepticism, I am sorry to say that I have not."
>
> Looking me earnestly in the face and placing his hand on my shoulder, he said, "You are wrong, Speed. Take all of this book upon reason that you can, and the balance on faith, and you will live and die a happier and better man."

Abraham Lincoln

52

"Thomas, because you have seen Me, you have believed. Blessed are those who have not seen and yet have believed."

JOHN 20:29

★ ★ ★ ★

If any of you lacks wisdom, let him ask of God, who gives to all liberally and without reproach, and it will be given to him. But let him ask in faith, with no doubting, for he who doubts is like a wave of the sea driven and tossed by the wind.

JAMES 1:5–6

★ ★ ★ ★

"Have faith in God. For assuredly, I say to you, whoever says to this mountain, 'Be removed and be cast into the sea,' and does not doubt in his heart, but believes that those things he says will be done, he will have whatever he says."

MARK 11:22–23

Finding Hope in Suffering

I n 1 Peter 4:12–13, the apostle Peter wrote to persecuted believers, encouraging them to persevere for the person and message of Christ. Peter provided them with a divine perspective on their trials so that they could endure them without wavering in their faith. Having been born again to a living hope, they are to imitate the Holy One who Himself suffered and to rely on His strong presence when they suffer.

As commander of the Allied forces in Europe during World War II and later president of the United States, Dwight D. Eisenhower also knew a great deal about the strength of men and women in difficult times. He said, "The spirit of man is more important than mere physical strength, and the spiritual fiber of a nation than its wealth. The Bible is endorsed by the ages. Our civilization is built upon its words. In no other book is there such a collection of inspired wisdom, reality, and hope."

Dwight D. Eisenhower

54

Beloved, do not think it strange concerning the fiery
trial which is to try you, as though some strange thing
happened to you; but rejoice to the extent that you
partake of Christ's sufferings, that when His glory is
revealed, you may also be glad with exceeding joy.

1 PETER 4:12–13

★ ★ ★ ★

And if children, then heirs—heirs of God and joint heirs
with Christ, if indeed we suffer with Him, that we may
also be glorified together. For I consider that the sufferings of this present time are not worthy to be compared
with the glory which shall be revealed in us.

ROMANS 8:17–18

★ ★ ★ ★

My brethren, count it all joy when you fall into various
trials, knowing that the testing of your faith produces
patience. But let patience have its perfect work, that you
may be perfect and complete, lacking nothing.

JAMES 1:2–4

In the 1885 Utah Territory case of *Murphy v. Ramsey,* the U.S. Supreme Court recognized the fundamental importance of the traditional institution of marriage:

> Every person who has a husband or wife living ... and marries another ... is guilty of polygamy, and shall be punished. ... For certainly no legislation can be supposed more wholesome and necessary in the founding of a free, self-governing commonwealth, fit to take rank as one of the coordinate States of the Union, than that which seeks to establish it on the basis of the idea of the family, as consisting in and springing from the union for life of one man and one woman in the holy estate of matrimony; the sure foundation of all that is stable and noble in our civilization; the best guaranty of that reverent morality which is the source of all beneficent progress in social and political improvement.

Let each man have his own wife, and let each woman have her own husband. Let the husband render to his wife the affection due her, and likewise also the wife to her husband.

1 CORINTHIANS 7:2–3

* * * *

"For this reason a man shall leave his father and mother and be joined to his wife, and the two shall become one flesh." This is a great mystery, but I speak concerning Christ and the church. Nevertheless let each one of you in particular so love his own wife as himself, and let the wife see that she respects her husband.

EPHESIANS 5:31–33

* * * *

Husbands, likewise, dwell with them with understanding, giving honor to the wife, as to the weaker vessel, and as being heirs together of the grace of life, that your prayers may not be hindered.

1 PETER 3:7

I n the 1892 case *The Church of the Holy Trinity v. United States*, the U.S. Supreme Court determined that an English minister was not a foreign laborer. The court considered America's Christian identity to be a strong support for concluding that Congress could not have intended to prohibit foreign ministers.

Justice David Josiah Brewer stated that the U.S. was a "Christian nation." The court had already demonstrated the country's religious character with eighty-seven examples from pre-Constitutional documents, historical practice, and colonial charters, that reveal religious roots.

> This is a religious people.... From the discovery of this continent to the present hour, there is a single voice making this affirmation....There is no dissonance in these declarations. There is a universal language pervading them all, having one meaning; they affirm and reaffirm that this is a religious nation. These are not individual sayings ... they speak the voice of the entire people.

Brewer later clarified his position: many American traditions are rooted in Christianity, but Christianity should not receive legal privileges or be established to the exclusion of other religions or irreligion.

David Josiah Brewer

58

But you are a chosen generation, a royal priesthood, a holy nation, His own special people, that you may proclaim the praises of Him who called you out of darkness into His marvelous light.

1 PETER 2:9

★ ★ ★ ★

Then it shall come to pass, because you listen to these judgments, and keep and do them, that the LORD your God will keep with you the covenant and the mercy which He swore to your fathers.

DEUTERONOMY 7:12

★ ★ ★ ★

And the Scripture, foreseeing that God would justify the Gentiles by faith, preached the gospel to Abraham beforehand, saying, "In you all the nations shall be blessed." So then those who are of faith are blessed with believing Abraham.

GALATIANS 3:8–9

Much has been written in recent years to try to dismiss the fact that America was founded upon the biblical principles of Judeo-Christianity, but all the revisionism in the world cannot change the facts. Anyone who examines the original writings, personal correspondence, biographies, and public statements of the individuals who were instrumental in the founding of America will find an abundance of quotations showing the profound extent to which their thinking and their lives were influenced by a Christian worldview.

That is not to say that all of the Founding Fathers were Christians. Such is not the case, but even those who were not Christians were deeply influenced by the principles of Christianity. We can easily get so distracted, wondering whether Benjamin Franklin or Thomas Jefferson ever put their personal faith in Jesus Christ, that we will easily miss the important fact that almost all the Founders thought from a biblical perspective, whether or not they believed.

"Because of your unbelief; for assuredly, I say to you, if you have faith as a mustard seed, you will say to this mountain, 'Move from here to there,' and it will move; and nothing will be impossible for you."

MATTHEW 17:20

* * * *

Therefore, having been justified by faith, we have peace with God through our Lord Jesus Christ, through whom also we have access by faith into this grace in which we stand, and rejoice in hope of the glory of God.

ROMANS 5:1–2

* * * *

And let us not grow weary while doing good, for in due season we shall reap if we do not lose heart.

GALATIANS 6:9

* * * *

Now faith is the substance of things hoped for, the evidence of things not seen.

HEBREWS 11:1

J edidiah Morse (1761–1826) was a pioneer American educator, clergyman, geographer, and father of Samuel Morse, inventor of the telegraph and Morse code. Jedidiah studied for the ministry at Yale and, in 1789, accepted a call to the First Church of Charlestown, Massachusetts. He was alarmed by how far the clergy had moved from doctrinal orthodoxy. In a 1799 sermon, he said the following:

> Our dangers are of two kinds, those which affect our religion, and those which affect our government. They are, however, so closely allied that they cannot, with propriety, be separated....
>
> To the kindly influence of Christianity we owe that degree of civil freedom, and political and social happiness ... mankind now enjoys. In proportion as the genuine effects of Christianity are diminished in any nation ... in the same proportion will the people of that nation recede from the blessings of genuine freedom.... It follows, that all efforts made to destroy the foundations of our holy religion, ultimately tend to the subversion also of our political freedom and happiness. Whenever the pillars of Christianity shall be overthrown, our present republican forms of government, and all the blessings which flow from them, must fall with them.

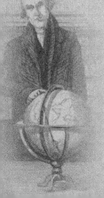

Jedidiah Morse

According to the grace of God which was given to me, as a wise master builder I have laid the foundation, and another builds on it. But let each one take heed how he builds on it. For no other foundation can anyone lay than that which is laid, which is Jesus Christ.

1 CORINTHIANS 3:10–11

* * * *

Nevertheless the solid foundation of God stands, having this seal: "The Lord knows those who are His," and, "Let everyone who names the name of Christ depart from iniquity."

2 TIMOTHY 2:19

* * * *

In the LORD I put my trust;
　How can you say to my soul,
　　"Flee as a bird to your mountain"? . . .
If the foundations are destroyed,
　What can the righteous do?

PSALM 11:1, 3

B etween 1957 and 1975, a heated part of the Cold War between the Soviet Union and the United States was competition in the realm of space exploration because of its potential military and technological applications, as well as its morale-boosting social benefits. The Soviets took the lead in the Space Race when they were the first to achieve a manned orbit of the earth in 1961. But on February 20, 1962, atop an Atlas rocket, Colonel John Glenn piloted the first American manned orbital mission aboard *Friendship 7*, circling the globe three times. Taking this step toward fulfilling America's political and scientific hopes and dreams, Glenn returned to Earth as virtually every American's hero.

In 1998, NASA invited John Glenn to join the space shuttle *Discovery* crew. On October 29, 1998, he became the oldest human, at the age of seventy-seven, to venture into space. As Glenn observed the heavens and Earth from the windows of *Discovery*, he said, "To look out at this kind of creation out here and not believe in God is to me impossible. It just strengthens my faith. I wish there were words to describe what it's like."

John Glenn

The heavens declare the glory of God;
    And the firmament shows His handiwork.

PSALM 19:1

* * * *

Let the heavens declare His righteousness,
    For God Himself is Judge.

PSALM 50:6

* * * *

The heavens are Yours, the earth also is Yours;
    The world and all its fullness, You have founded them.

PSALM 89:11

* * * *

Before the mountains were brought forth,
    Or ever You had formed the earth and the world,
    Even from everlasting to everlasting, You are God.

PSALM 90:2

Major General Henry Lee said about George Washington, "First in war, first in peace, and first in the hearts of his countrymen." Emerging as the most significant leader in the founding of the United States, he was the essential man, the American Moses, the Father of the Country. At the three crossroads in the establishment of the nation, he led our troops to victory in the Revolutionary War, superintended the Constitutional Convention, and was unanimously elected first president.

How can such greatness be embodied in one man? Washington was surrounded by a host of other courageous leaders, brilliant thinkers, passionate orators, and gifted writers—Franklin, Jefferson, Patrick Henry, John and Samuel Adams, Hamilton, Madison—almost all of whom were far more educated than he. Yet Washington always led the way.

While much has often been made of his physical stature (six foot two) and his courage, charisma, energy, vision, and calm demeanor, it was his moral character most historical sources commonly cite as the reason for his emergence. Combine his sterling character and his genius in the area of leadership, and here was a man who could be trusted to lead.

George Washington

Come now, therefore, and I will send you to Pharaoh
that you may bring My people, the children of Israel,
out of Egypt.

EXODUS 3:10

★ ★ ★ ★

Search me, O God, and know my heart;
    Try me, and know my anxieties;
And see if there is any wicked way in me,
    And lead me in the way everlasting.

PSALM 139:23–24

★ ★ ★ ★

Judge me, O LORD, according to my righteousness,
And according to my integrity within me.

PSALM 7:8

★ ★ ★ ★

Examine me, O LORD, and prove me;
    Try my mind and my heart.
For Your lovingkindness is before my eyes,
    And I have walked in Your truth.

PSALM 26:2–3

On July 2, 1776, as the Continental Congress was meeting in Philadelphia to declare independence, Commander in Chief George Washington was gathering his troops on Long Island to meet the British in battle in and around New York City. That day he wrote in the General Orders to his men these memorable words declaring that we, as a nation, serve under God:

> The time is now near at hand which must probably determine whether Americans are to be freemen or slaves. . . . The fate of unborn millions will now depend, under God, on the courage and conduct of this army. Our cruel and unrelenting enemy leaves us no choice but a brave resistance, or the most abject submission; this is all we can expect.
>
> We have therefore to resolve to conquer or die. . . .
>
> Let us therefore rely upon the goodness of the cause, and the aid of the Supreme Being, in whose hands victory is, to animate and encourage us to great and noble actions. The eyes of all our countrymen are now upon us, and we shall have their blessings and praises, if happily we are the instruments of saving them from the tyranny meditated against them. Let us therefore . . . show the whole world that a freeman contending for liberty on his own ground is superior to any slavish mercenary on earth.

George Washington

"But he who is greatest among you shall be your servant. And whoever exalts himself will be humbled, and he who humbles himself will be exalted."

MATTHEW 23:11–12

* * * *

"Then the righteous will answer Him, saying, 'Lord, when did we see You hungry and feed You, or thirsty and give You drink? When did we see You a stranger and take You in, or naked and clothe You? Or when did we see You sick, or in prison, and come to You?' And the King will answer and say to them, 'Assuredly, I say to you, inasmuch as you did it to one of the least of these My brethren, you did it to Me.'"

MATTHEW 25:37–40

* * * *

Therefore, since we are receiving a kingdom which cannot be shaken, let us have grace, by which we may serve God acceptably with reverence and godly fear.

HEBREWS 12:28

C onsidered one of the greatest orators in American
history, Daniel Webster (1782–1852) served as
a U.S. congressman and senator as well as secretary of
state for three different presidents. The following is from
a speech given before the Historical Society of New York
on February 23, 1852:

> If we and our posterity shall be true to the
> Christian religion, if we and they shall live
> always in the fear of God, and shall respect His
> commandments, if we and they shall maintain
> just moral sentiments and such conscientious
> convictions of duty as shall control the heart and
> life, we may have the highest hopes of the future
> fortunes of our country. . . .
>
> But if we and our posterity reject religious
> institutions and authority, violate the rules
> of eternal justice, trifle with the injunctions
> of morality, and recklessly destroy the
> political constitution which holds us
> together, no man can tell how sudden a
> catastrophe may overwhelm us.

Daniel Webster

To do righteousness and justice
    Is more acceptable to the LORD than sacrifice.

PROVERBS 21:3

★ ★ ★ ★

He who follows righteousness and mercy
    Finds life, righteousness and honor.

PROVERBS 21:21

★ ★ ★ ★

He who has a generous eye will be blessed,
    For he gives of his bread to the poor.

PROVERBS 22:9

★ ★ ★ ★

My son, if your heart is wise,
    My heart will rejoice—indeed, I myself;
Yes, my inmost being will rejoice
    When your lips speak right things.

PROVERBS 23:15–16

Benjamin Silliman (1779–1864), an American physicist, chemist, and geologist, founded and edited the *American Journal of Science and Arts*. Hear his perspective on science and Scripture:

> The relation of geology, as well as astronomy, to the Bible, when both are well understood, is that of perfect harmony. The Bible nowhere limits the age of the globe, while its chronology assigns a recent origin to the human race; and geology ... confirms that Genesis presents a true statement of the progress of the terrestrial arrangements and of the introduction of living beings in the order in which their fossil remains are found entombed in the strata.
>
> The Word and the works of God cannot conflict, and the more they are studied the more perfect will their harmony appear.

In the beginning was the Word, and the Word was with God, and the Word was God. He was in the beginning with God. All things were made through Him, and without Him nothing was made that was made.

JOHN 1:1–3

★ ★ ★ ★

And the Word became flesh and dwelt among us, and we beheld His glory, the glory as of the only begotten of the Father, full of grace and truth.

JOHN 1:14

★ ★ ★ ★

Let the word of Christ dwell in you richly in all wisdom, teaching and admonishing one another in psalms and hymns and spiritual songs, singing with grace in your hearts to the Lord. And whatever you do in word or deed, do all in the name of the Lord Jesus, giving thanks to God the Father through Him.

COLOSSIANS 3:16–17

Scripture's unifying theme is God's unchanging covenant with His people. When Israel stayed true to God's Word and His will, He blessed the nation with prosperity. When the people disobeyed God, they faced some stiff consequences. Then in Nehemiah 9, after Ezra read the law, the people confessed their sin and boldly reaffirmed their loyalty to God's covenant.

On March 4, 1933, in his first inaugural address and at the beginning of the Great Depression, President Franklin D. Roosevelt spoke a bold word of encouragement to his fellow citizens: "Let me assert my firm belief that the only thing we have to fear is fear itself. . . . We face arduous days that lie before us in the warm courage of national unity; with the clear consciousness of seeking old and precious moral values." Beseeching God's blessing, the president added, "May He protect each and every one of us! May He guide me in the days to come!" FDR's leadership would be a decisive factor in keeping America's resolve strong throughout the years of the Depression and the world war that followed.

Franklin D. Roosevelt

He who walks righteously and speaks uprightly,
 He who despises the gain of oppressions,
 Who gestures with his hands, refusing bribes,
 Who stops his ears from hearing of bloodshed,
 And shuts his eyes from seeing evil:
 He will dwell on high;
 His place of defense will be the fortress of rocks;
 Bread will be given him,
 His water will be sure.

ISAIAH 33:15–16

★ ★ ★ ★

For this is God,
 Our God forever and ever;
 He will be our guide
 Even to death.

PSALM 48:14

★ ★ ★ ★

I will instruct you and teach you in the way you
      should go;
 I will guide you with My eye.

PSALM 32:8

In his inaugural address on March 5, 1877, Rutherford B. Hayes, the nineteenth president of the United States (1877–1881), stated the following:

> Looking for the guidance of that Divine Hand by which the destinies of nations and individuals are shaped, I call upon you, Senators, Representatives, judges, fellow citizens, here and everywhere, to unite with me in an earnest effort to secure to our country the blessings, not only of material property, but of justice, peace, and union—a union depending not upon the constraint of force but upon the loving devotion of a free people; and that all things may be so ordered and settled upon the best and surest foundations that peace and happiness, truth and justice, religion and piety, may be established among us for all generations.

The LORD bless you and keep you;
The LORD make His face shine upon you,
   And be gracious to you;
The LORD lift up His countenance upon you,
   And give you peace.

NUMBERS 6:24–26

* * * *

Let my cry come before You, O LORD;
   Give me understanding according to Your word.
Let my supplication come before You;
   Deliver me according to Your word. . . .
Let Your hand become my help,
   For I have chosen Your precepts.

PSALM 119:169–170, 173

* * * *

Establish Your word to Your servant,
   Who is devoted to fearing You.
Turn away my reproach which I dread,
   For Your judgments are good.
Behold, I long for Your precepts;
   Revive me in Your righteousness.

PSALM 119:38–40

The Gettysburg Address

The Battle of Gettysburg (July 1–3, 1863) resulted in over 51,000 deaths, the largest number of casualties in the Civil War. Abraham Lincoln's November 19, 1863, address at the dedication of the Soldiers' National Cemetery in Gettysburg is regarded as one of the greatest speeches in American history:

Fourscore and seven years ago our fathers brought forth on this continent a new nation, conceived in liberty and dedicated to the proposition that all men are created equal. Now we are engaged in a great civil war, testing whether that nation or any nation so conceived and so dedicated can long endure. We are met on a great battlefield of that war. We have come to dedicate a portion of that field as a final resting place for those who here gave their lives that that nation might live. . . . It is for us the living rather to be dedicated here to the unfinished work which they who fought here have thus far so nobly advanced. It is rather for us to be here dedicated to the great task remaining before us . . . that we here highly resolve that these dead shall not have died in vain, that this nation under God shall have a new birth of freedom, and that government of the people, by the people, for the people shall not perish from the earth.

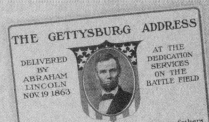

I n Colossians—perhaps the most Christ-centered book in the Bible—the apostle Paul refuted a threatening heresy that devalued Christ by explaining that believers are risen with Christ and are to put off the old man and put on the new, which will result in holiness in all relationships. Paul stressed the preeminence of Christ and the completeness of the salvation He provides. Paul countered false teaching with his presentation of Jesus. A proper view of Christ is always the most powerful antidote to heresy.

Just as the Colossians needed to guard the truth of the gospel, so we need to guard our country. President Calvin Coolidge said:

> The issues of the world must be met and met squarely. The forces of evil do not disdain preparation, they are always prepared and always preparing.... The welfare of America, the cause of civilization will forever require the contribution, of some part of the life, of all our citizens, to the natural, the necessary, and the inevitable demand for the defense of the right and the truth.

Calvin Coolidge

"If you abide in My word, you are My disciples indeed. And you shall know the truth, and the truth shall make you free."

JOHN 8:31–32

★ ★ ★ ★

"I am the way, the truth, and the life. No one comes to the Father except through Me. If you had known Me, you would have known My Father also; and from now on you know Him and have seen Him."

JOHN 14:6–7

★ ★ ★ ★

"Let each one of you speak truth with his neighbor," for we are members of one another.

EPHESIANS 4:25

★ ★ ★ ★

"Sanctify them by Your truth. Your word is truth. As You sent Me into the world, I also have sent them into the world. And for their sakes I sanctify Myself, that they also may be sanctified by the truth."

JOHN 17:17–19

A wise person once said, "Freedom is never free."
Nathan Hale (1755–1776) was a schoolteacher
when the Revolutionary War broke out in April 1775.
After hearing about the siege of Boston, Hale joined his
five brothers in the fight for independence.

Hale fought under General George Washington in
New York as British General William Howe began a
military buildup on Long Island. When Washington
asked for a volunteer to spy behind enemy lines, Hale
stepped forward. For a week he gathered information on
the position of British troops, but he was captured while
returning. Because of the incriminating papers Hale
possessed, the British knew he was a spy. Howe ordered
the twenty-year-old Hale to be hanged the following day
without a trial.

Patriot Nathan Hale was hanged on September 22,
1776. Before he gave his life for his country, he made a
short speech, ending with these famous and inspiring
words: "I only regret that I have but one life to lose for
my country."

As John Quincy Adams said, "You will never know
how much it has cost my generation to preserve your
freedom. I hope you will make good use of it." We must
do all we can to protect the freedoms that generations
past have entrusted to us.

"This is My commandment, that you love one another as I have loved you. Greater love has no one than this, than to lay down one's life for his friends."

JOHN 15:12–13

★ ★ ★ ★

Happy is he who has the God of Jacob for his help,
    Whose hope is in the LORD his God,
Who made heaven and earth,
    The sea, and all that is in them;
    Who keeps truth forever,
Who executes justice for the oppressed,
    Who gives food to the hungry.
    The LORD gives freedom to the prisoners.

PSALM 146:5–7

★ ★ ★ ★

What then shall we say to these things? If God is for us, who can be against us? He who did not spare His own Son, but delivered Him up for us all, how shall He not with Him also freely give us all things?

ROMANS 8:31–32

The Joy of Worship

The book of Psalms is a profoundly rich and personal guide to worship, praise, prayer, meditation, and even instruction about God. Containing some of the most beautiful poetry ever penned, the psalms can help us express our deepest needs, thoughts, and desires to our heavenly Father—in times of great joy as well as in times of great sorrow.

Fanny Crosby (1820–1915), one of America's most beloved hymn writers, no doubt received much inspiration and tutoring in song from time spent in the book of Psalms. Blind from infancy, she nevertheless went on to pen more than eight thousand songs of praise to God, including such classic hymns as "Near the Cross," "Praise Him, Praise Him," and "To God Be the Glory." The chorus of one of her most well-known hymns, "Blessed Assurance," sums up the theme of Psalms:

> *This is my story, this is my song,*
> *Praising my Savior all the day long;*
> *This is my story, this is my song,*
> *Praising my Savior all the day long.*

Oh come, let us worship and bow down;
    Let us kneel before the LORD our Maker.
For He is our God,
    And we are the people of His pasture,
    And the sheep of His hand.

PSALM 95:6–7

* * * *

Give to the LORD the glory due His name;
Bring an offering, and come before Him.
Oh, worship the LORD in the beauty of holiness!

1 CHRONICLES 16:29

* * * *

"But the hour is coming, and now is, when the true worshipers will worship the Father in spirit and truth; for the Father is seeking such to worship Him. God is Spirit, and those who worship Him must worship in spirit and truth."

JOHN 4:23–24

In the 1952 case *Zorach v. Clauson*, the Supreme Court upheld the New York City school district practice of releasing students during school hours for religious instruction:

> The First Amendment ... does not say that in every respect there shall be a separation of Church and State. Rather ... there shall be no concert or union or dependency one on the other. ... Otherwise the state and religion would be aliens to each other. ...
>
> Municipalities would not be permitted to render police or fire protection to religious groups. ... Prayers in our legislative halls; the appeals to the Almighty in the messages of the Chief Executive; "so help me God" in our courtroom oaths ... would be flouting the First Amendment. ...
>
> When the state ... cooperates with religious authorities by adjusting the schedule of public events ... it follows the best of our traditions. For it then respects the religious nature of our people and accommodates the public service to their spiritual needs. ... We cannot read into the Bill of Rights such a philosophy of hostility to religion.

Thomas Paine

Only take heed to yourself, and diligently keep yourself, lest you forget the things your eyes have seen, and lest they depart from your heart all the days of your life. And teach them to your children and your grandchildren.

DEUTERONOMY 4:9

* * * *

And these words which I command you today shall be in your heart. You shall teach them diligently to your children, and shall talk of them when you sit in your house, when you walk by the way, when you lie down, and when you rise up. You shall bind them as a sign on your hand, and they shall be as frontlets between your eyes. You shall write them on the doorposts of your house and on your gates.

DEUTERONOMY 6:6–9

* * * *

Teach me Your way, O LORD,
    And lead me in a smooth path, because of
        my enemies.

PSALM 27:11

America's rich history is filled with accounts of men and women who left the comfort and familiarity of their homes and families in search of greater freedom and opportunity. With hearts set on adventure, these early pioneers braved hardships and hazards to claim their personal "promised land." And that choice required courage, determination, and faith in God.

The book of Numbers recounts a similar grand adventure, of God preparing His own people to conquer the land of milk and honey that He had promised them generations earlier. Before they can succeed, however, the people of Israel must deal with the fear and doubt that grip them. God required—and He requires it today—that those called by His Name put their faith in Him alone. Numbers shows the process by which He brought His people to that place of trust and led them into a place of blessing.

Independence

Trust in the LORD with all your heart,
    And lean not on your own understanding;
In all your ways acknowledge Him,
    And He shall direct your paths.

PROVERBS 3:5–6

* * * *

And it shall come to pass
That just as you were a curse among the nations,
O house of Judah and house of Israel,
So I will save you, and you shall be a blessing.
Do not fear,
Let your hands be strong.

ZECHARIAH 8:13

* * * *

Blessed is the man
    Who walks not in the counsel of the ungodly,
    Nor stands in the path of sinners,
    Nor sits in the seat of the scornful;
But his delight is in the law of the LORD,
    And in His law he meditates day and night.

PSALM 1:1–2

The fourth president of the United States and "Chief Architect of the Constitution," James Madison (1751–1836), wrote the following:

> The religion then of every man must be left to the conviction and conscience of every man; and it is the right of every man to exercise it as these may dictate. This right is in its nature an unalienable right. It is unalienable, because the opinions of men, depending only on the evidence contemplated by their own minds cannot follow the dictates of other men: It is unalienable also, because what is here a right toward men, is a duty toward the Creator. It is the duty of every man to render to the Creator such homage and such only as he believes to be acceptable to him. This duty is precedent, both in order of time and in degree of obligation, to the claims of civil society. Before any man can be considered as a member of civil society, he must be considered as a subject of the Governor of the Universe.

James Madison

Remember now your Creator in the days of your youth,
Before the difficult days come,
And the years draw near when you say,
"I have no pleasure in them."

ECCLESIASTES 12:1

* * * *

Have you not known?
Have you not heard?
The everlasting God, the LORD,
The Creator of the ends of the earth,
Neither faints nor is weary.
His understanding is unsearchable.
He gives power to the weak,
And to those who have no might He increases strength.

ISAIAH 40:28–29

* * * *

Therefore let those who suffer according to the will of God commit their souls to Him in doing good, as to a faithful Creator.

1 PETER 4:19

The Fundamentals

I n the late nineteenth and early twentieth centuries, conservative evangelical Christians began to reject the growing influence of modernism, especially the movement toward a social, humanistic gospel. Relying on *The Fundamentals*, written by prominent pastors and scholars in the 1910s, these believers affirmed Christian beliefs being questioned by growing liberalism.

The first formulation of these beliefs can be traced to the Niagara Bible Conference. In 1910, the General Assembly of the Presbyterian Church outlined "five fundamentals":

1. Inerrancy of the Scriptures
2. The virgin birth and the deity of Jesus Christ (Isaiah 7:14)
3. The doctrine of substitutionary atonement by God's grace and through human faith (Hebrews 9)
4. The bodily resurrection of Jesus (Matthew 28)
5. The authenticity of Christ's miracles

Many strongly conservative churches combined their religious views with social and political action. The movement's plain and powerful teaching revived the American church. Colleges, seminaries, missionary agencies, homes for troubled youths and the aged, and the Christian school movement have followed, as have the Christian publishing, radio, and television industries. These efforts remain a major force in religious America.

"I am the true vine, and My Father is the vinedresser. Every branch in Me that does not bear fruit He takes away; and every branch that bears fruit He prunes, that it may bear more fruit. . . .

"I am the vine, you are the branches. He who abides in Me, and I in him, bears much fruit; for without Me you can do nothing."

JOHN 15:1–2, 5

* * * *

Finally, brethren, whatever things are true, whatever things are noble, whatever things are just,
whatever things are pure, whatever things are lovely, whatever things are of good report, if there is any virtue and if there is anything praiseworthy—meditate on these things. The things which you learned and received and heard and saw in me, these do, and the God of peace will be with you.

PHILIPPIANS 4:8–9

P atrick Henry (1736–1799) was one of the most
passionate and fiery advocates of the American
Revolution. Many have compared him to an Old
Testament prophet in his powerful denunciations of
corruption in government officials and his defense of
the colonists' rights. Elected to the Virginia legislature in
1775, he rallied Virginia into military preparedness.

Rebellion against unjust taxes had begun, and the
British had posted troops throughout the colonies and
warships in the harbors. On March 23, 1775, during
the Second Virginia Convention's debates on whether
to declare independence or negotiate with the British,
Patrick Henry called upon his countrymen to trust God:

> Sirs, we shall not fight our battles alone. There
> is a just God who presides over the destinies of
> nations, and who will raise up friends to fight our
> battles for us. The battle, sir, is not to the strong
> alone; it is to the vigilant, the active, the brave.

Hear his passionate conclusion:

> Is life so dear, or peace so sweet, as to be
> purchased at the price of chains and slavery?
> Forbid it, Almighty God! I know not what
> course others may take; but as for me, give me
> liberty or give me death!

Patrick Henry

Choose for yourselves this day whom you will serve, whether the gods which your fathers served that were on the other side of the River, or the gods of the Amorites, in whose land you dwell. But as for me and my house, we will serve the LORD.

JOSHUA 24:15

★ ★ ★ ★

Therefore, having been justified by faith, we have peace with God through our Lord Jesus Christ, through whom also we have access by faith into this grace in which we stand, and rejoice in hope of the glory of God.

ROMANS 5:1–2

★ ★ ★ ★

"You did not choose Me, but I chose you and appointed you that you should go and bear fruit, and that your fruit should remain, that whatever you ask the Father in My name He may give you. These things I command you, that you love one another."

JOHN 15:16–17

One-time director of NASA and "Father of the American Space Program" Wernher von Braun stated the following in a May 1974 article:

> One cannot be exposed to the law and order of the universe without concluding that there must be design and purpose behind it all. . . . The better we understand the intricacies of the universe and all it harbors, the more reason we have found to marvel at the inherent design upon which it is based. . . .
>
> To be forced to believe only one conclusion— that everything in the universe happened by chance—would violate the very objectivity of science itself. . . . What random process could produce the brains of a man or the system of the human eye? . . .
>
> [Evolutionists] challenge science to prove the existence of God. But must we really light a candle to see the sun? . . . They say they cannot visualize a Designer. Well, can a physicist visualize an electron? . . . What strange rationale makes some physicists accept the inconceivable electron as real while refusing to accept the reality of a Designer on the grounds that they cannot conceive Him?

Wernher von Braun

In the beginning was the Word, and the Word was with God, and the Word was God. He was in the beginning with God. All things were made through Him, and without Him nothing was made that was made. In Him was life, and the life was the light of men.

JOHN 1:1–4

* * * *

In the beginning God created the heavens and the earth. The earth was without form, and void; and darkness was on the face of the deep. And the Spirit of God was hovering over the face of the waters. Then God said, "Let there be light"; and there was light.

GENESIS 1:1–3

* * * *

He is the image of the invisible God, the firstborn over all creation. For by Him all things were created that are in heaven and that are on earth, visible and invisible, whether thrones or dominions or principalities or powers. All things were created through Him and for Him.

COLOSSIANS 1:15–16

According to the Declaration of Independence, the American colonists were determined to defend "the laws of nature and of nature's God." This phrase defines the key principle upon which the Founders stood. The *laws of nature* meant the will of God for man as revealed to man's reason. However, because man is fallen and his reason does not always comprehend this law, God gave us the Bible to make His law absolutely clear.

The churches in the colonies became a voice of freedom, stirring the fires of liberty by telling the colonists that the British government was usurping their God-given rights and that the king and Parliament were violating the laws of God. The Founding Fathers were convinced that it was their sacred duty to start a revolution in order to uphold the law of God against the unjust and oppressive laws of men. This fight for political liberty was seen as a sacred cause because civil liberty is an inalienable right, according to God's natural law.

You shall walk after the LORD your God and fear Him, and keep His commandments and obey His voice; you shall serve Him and hold fast to Him.

DEUTERONOMY 13:4

* * * *

For this is the will of God, that by doing good you may put to silence the ignorance of foolish men—as free, yet not using liberty as a cloak for vice, but as bondservants of God. Honor all people. Love the brotherhood. Fear God. Honor the king.

1 PETER 2:15–17

* * * *

But you are a chosen generation, a royal priesthood, a holy nation, His own special people, that you may proclaim the praises of Him who called you out of darkness into His marvelous light; who once were not a people but are now the people of God, who had not obtained mercy but now have obtained mercy.

1 PETER 2:9–10

F ew accounts in the Bible paint a picture of loyalty the way the story of Jonathan and David's friendship does. Despite the attempts of King Saul—his father—to kill David, Jonathan pledges his loyalty to David. Jonathan is loyal to his principles and his friend in the face of the greatest opposition.

During the Revolutionary War, there were far more Loyalists (American colonists who remained loyal to the British monarchy) than one might think. According to historian Robert Calhoun, "best estimates put the proportion of adult white male Loyalists somewhere between 15 and 20 percent [approximately five hundred thousand men]. Approximately half the colonists of European ancestry tried to avoid involvement in the struggle. The Patriots received active support from perhaps 40 to 45 percent of the white populace, and at most no more than a bare majority." Some of the Loyalists returned to Europe, but many remained in the colonies, fighting against the Founding Fathers and influencing others to follow in their steps. In spite of this opposition, the Patriots continued to fight for what they believed was God's will.

Let your heart therefore be loyal to the LORD our God,
to walk in His statutes and keep His commandments, as
at this day.

1 KINGS 8:61

★ ★ ★ ★

Commit your way to the LORD,
    Trust also in Him,
    And He shall bring it to pass.
He shall bring forth your righteousness as the light,
    And your justice as the noonday.

PSALM 37:5–6

★ ★ ★ ★

Oh, love the LORD, all you His saints!
    For the LORD preserves the faithful,
    And fully repays the proud person.
Be of good courage,
    And He shall strengthen your heart,
    All you who hope in the LORD.

PSALM 31:23–24

In anguish over the ravages of civil war, President Abraham Lincoln declared a National Fast Day on March 30, 1863:

> We have been the recipients of the choicest bounties of Heaven; we have been preserved these many years in peace and prosperity; we have grown in numbers, wealth, and power as no other nation has ever grown. But we have forgotten God. We have forgotten the gracious hand which preserved us in peace and multiplied and enriched and strengthened us, and we have vainly imagined, in the deceitfulness of our hearts, that all these blessings were produced by some superior wisdom and virtue of our own. Intoxicated with unbroken success, we have become too self-sufficient to feel the necessity of redeeming and preserving grace, too proud to pray to the God that made us. It behooves us, then, to humble ourselves before the offended Power, to confess our national sins, and to pray for clemency and forgiveness.

President Abraham Lincoln reading the Bible to his son

102

The humble He guides in justice,
    And the humble He teaches His way.
All the paths of the LORD are mercy and truth,
    To such as keep His covenant and His testimonies.

PSALM 25:9–10

★ ★ ★ ★

For I know the thoughts that I think toward you, says
the LORD, thoughts of peace and not of evil, to give you
a future and a hope. Then you will call upon Me and go
and pray to Me, and I will listen to you. And you will
seek Me and find Me, when you search for Me with all
your heart.

JEREMIAH 29:11–13

★ ★ ★ ★

If we say that we have no sin, we deceive ourselves, and
the truth is not in us. If we confess our sins, He is faithful and just to forgive us our sins and to cleanse us from
all unrighteousness.

1 JOHN 1:8–9

Captain Russell Rippetoe was serving in Operation Iraqi Freedom in March 2003. Previously, while serving in Afghanistan, Rippetoe saw men die, which brought a renewal to his Christian faith and a new passion for the Bible. On the chain around his neck, he wore a "Shield of Strength," a one-by-two-inch emblem displaying a U.S. flag on one side and words from Joshua 1:9 on the other.

On April 3, 2003, Rippetoe's company was manning a nighttime checkpoint near the Hadithah Dam when a vehicle approached. Suddenly, a woman jumped out and cried, "I'm hungry. I need food and water!" Protecting his men, Rippetoe gave the order to hold back as he moved toward the woman to see how he could help. When she hesitated, the driver detonated a car bomb that killed Captain Rippetoe, Sergeant Nino Livaudais, and Specialist Ryan Long and wounded several others.

Rippetoe believed the ancient words of Joshua 1:9: "The LORD your God is with you wherever you go." Rippetoe, who died trying to help someone, was the first casualty of the Iraq conflict to be buried at Arlington National Cemetery.

Arlington National Cemetary

The LORD is my light and my salvation;
    Whom shall I fear?

PSALM 27:1

★ ★ ★ ★

For His anger is but for a moment,
    His favor is for life;
    Weeping may endure for a night,
    But joy comes in the morning.

PSALM 30:5

★ ★ ★ ★

The LORD is my strength and my shield;
    My heart trusted in Him, and I am helped;
    Therefore my heart greatly rejoices,
    And with my song I will praise Him.

PSALM 28:7

Warren Earl Burger, chief justice of the U.S. Supreme Court from 1969 to 1986, delivered the court's opinion in the 1982 case of *Marsh v. Chambers*, regarding chaplains opening legislative sessions with prayer:

The men who wrote the First Amendment religion clause did not view paid legislative chaplains and opening prayers as a violation of that amendment . . .

> It can hardly be thought that in the same week the members of the first Congress voted to appoint and pay a chaplain for each House and also voted to approve the draft of the First Amendment . . . [that] they intended to forbid what they had just declared acceptable. . . .
>
> The legislature by majority vote invites a clergyman to give a prayer, neither the inviting nor the giving nor the hearing of the prayer is making a law. On this basis alone . . . the sayings of prayers, per se, in the legislative halls at the opening session is not prohibited by the First and Fourteenth Amendments.

Warren Earl Burger

Give heed to the voice of my cry,
  My King and my God,
  For to You I will pray.
My voice You shall hear in the morning, O LORD;
  In the morning I will direct it to You,
  And I will look up.

PSALM 5:2–3

* * * *

Be anxious for nothing, but in everything by prayer
and supplication, with thanksgiving, let your requests
be made known to God; and the peace of God, which
surpasses all understanding, will guard your hearts and
minds through Christ Jesus.

PHILIPPIANS 4:6–7

* * * *

Let every soul be subject to the governing authorities.
For there is no authority except from God, and the
authorities that exist are appointed by God.

ROMANS 13:1

Benjamin Franklin Butler (1795–1858), U.S. attorney general under President Andrew Jackson, knew the value of God's Word:

> He is truly happy, whatever may be his temporal condition, who can call God his Father in the full assurance of faith and hope. And amid all his trials, conflicts, and doubts, the feeblest Christian is still comparatively happy; because cheered by the hope . . . that the hour is coming when he shall be delivered from "this body of sin and death" and in the vision of his Redeemer . . . approximate to the . . . felicity of angels.
>
> Not only does the Bible inculcate, with sanctions of the highest import, a system of the purest morality, but in the person and character of our Blessed Savior it exhibits a tangible illustration of that system.
>
> In Him we have set before us . . . a model of feeling and action, adapted to all times, places, and circumstances; and combining so much of wisdom, benevolence, and holiness, that none can fathom its sublimity; and yet, presented in a form so simple, that even a child may be made to understand and taught to love it.

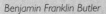

Benjamin Franklin Butler

Now thanks be to God who always leads us in triumph in Christ, and through us diffuses the fragrance of His knowledge in every place. For we are to God the fragrance of Christ among those who are being saved and among those who are perishing.

2 CORINTHIANS 2:14–15

★ ★ ★ ★

Brethren, if a man is overtaken in any trespass, you who are spiritual restore such a one in a spirit of gentleness, considering yourself lest you also be tempted. Bear one another's burdens, and so fulfill the law of Christ.

GALATIANS 6:1–2

★ ★ ★ ★

Brethren, I do not count myself to have apprehended; but one thing I do, forgetting those things which are behind and reaching forward to those things which are ahead, I press toward the goal for the prize of the upward call of God in Christ Jesus.

PHILIPPIANS 3:13–14

A dviser to Presidents Roosevelt and Taft, educator
Booker T. Washington (1856–1915) founded
Tuskegee Institute, a vocational school for African-
Americans. Its graduates became leaders and educators
across the nation.

Born a slave, Washington worked in Virginia coal
mines and salt furnaces starting at age nine. Determined
to get an education, at sixteen he went to Hampton
Institute, an industrial school for African-Americans.
Graduating with honors in just three years, he joined
the faculty and was soon asked to lead a new school
in Tuskegee. Starting with an abandoned church, he
built Tuskegee Institute into a school of 107 buildings
with over fifteen hundred students and more than two
hundred teachers and professors—all by 1915.

Wanting to produce businessmen, farmers, and
teachers, Washington offered traditional academic
courses; industry and trade skills like bricklaying, forestry,
sewing, cooking, and agriculture; and the training of
"head, hand, and heart," an emphasis on high moral
character shaped by the Christian faith. Washington
wrote that "the Christ-like work which the
Church of all denominations in
America has done" convinced
him of the value of the
Christian life.

He who follows righteousness and mercy
Finds life, righteousness, and honor.

PROVERBS 21:21

* * * *

For we are God's fellow workers; you are God's field, you
are God's building. According to the grace of God which
was given to me, as a wise master builder I have laid the
foundation, and another builds on it. But let each one take
heed how he builds on it. For no other foundation can
anyone lay than that which is laid, which is Jesus Christ.

1 CORINTHIANS 3:9–11

* * * *

Therefore, if anyone is in Christ, he is a new creation;
old things have passed away; behold, all things have
become new. Now all things are of God, who has
reconciled us to Himself through Jesus Christ, and has
given us the ministry of reconciliation, that is, that God
was in Christ reconciling the world to Himself, not
imputing their trespasses to them, and has committed to
us the word of reconciliation.

2 CORINTHIANS 5:17–19

A Godly Legacy

At age six, Henry John Heinz (1844–1919) helped his mother tend a small family garden. At twelve, he was working more than three acres and making deliveries to Pittsburgh grocery stores. He went on to found a company that he named 57 Varieties. Today the H. J. Heinz Company sells more than thirteen hundred products, ranging from ketchup to baby food.

Heinz's company pioneered safe and sanitary food preparation and was ahead of its time in employee relations, providing free medical benefits. Women held supervisory positions. Henry Heinz was also very involved in promoting Sunday school in Pittsburgh and around the world.

In his will, Heinz said, "I desire to set forth at the very beginning of this will, . . . a confession of my faith in Jesus Christ as my Savior. I also desire to bear witness to the fact that throughout my life, . . . I have been wonderfully sustained by my faith in God through Jesus Christ. This legacy was left me by my consecrated mother, a woman of strong faith, and to it I attribute any success I have attained."

Henry John Heinz

Fear not, for I am with you;
Be not dismayed, for I am your God.
I will strengthen you,
Yes, I will help you,
I will uphold you with My righteous right hand.

ISAIAH 41:10

★ ★ ★ ★

"Blessed are you when they revile and persecute you,
and say all kinds of evil against you falsely for My sake.
Rejoice and be exceedingly glad, for great is your reward
in heaven, for so they persecuted the prophets who were
before you."

MATTHEW 5:11–12

★ ★ ★ ★

"Let your light so shine before men, that they may see
your good works and glorify your Father in heaven."

MATTHEW 5:16

Perhaps surprisingly, New England ministers played a key role in rallying popular support for war against England. They pressed their congregations to overthrow King George because they believed that rebellion to tyrants was obedience to God. From many pulpits, ministers recruited troops and strengthened them for battle.

These church leaders knew that the Bible places great emphasis on due submission to civil authorities (Romans 13), but they noted that many passages approve resistance to ungodly authority (Acts 5:29).

It is, therefore, no coincidence that one of watchwords of the American Revolution was "No King But King Jesus." Most of the patriots found in their faith and in God's Word the courage to risk their lives and properties in order to break the tyranny of an unjust human authority. According to their Christian worldview, obedience to God took precedence over loyalty to country or government: their primary allegiance was to the Lord Jesus Christ.

Now it shall come to pass, if you diligently obey the voice of the LORD your God, to observe carefully all His commandments which I command you today, that the LORD your God will set you high above all nations of the earth. And all these blessings shall come upon you and overtake you, because you obey the voice of the LORD your God.

DEUTERONOMY 28:1–2

★ ★ ★ ★

But this is what I commanded them, saying, "Obey My voice, and I will be your God, and you shall be My people. And walk in all the ways that I have commanded you, that it may be well with you."

JEREMIAH 7:23

★ ★ ★ ★

But Peter and the other apostles answered and said: "We ought to obey God rather than men. The God of our fathers raised up Jesus whom you murdered by hanging on a tree. Him God has exalted to His right hand to be Prince and Savior, to give repentance to Israel and forgiveness of sins."

ACTS 5:29–31

Faith of the Founders

No people can be bound to
ACKNOWLEDGE AND ADORE THE INVISIBLE
HAND WHICH CONDUCTS THE AFFAIRS OF MEN
more than those of the United States.

GEORGE WASHINGTON | *April 30, 1789*

My only hope of salvation is in the infinite, transcendent love of God manifested to the world by the death of His Son upon the cross. Nothing but His blood will wash away my sins. I rely exclusively upon it. Come, Lord Jesus! Come quickly!

BENJAMIN RUSH | *signer of the Declaration of Independence*

I shall need, too, the favor of that Being in whose hands we are . . . and to whose goodness I ask you to join in supplications with me.

THOMAS JEFFERSON | *March 4, 1805*

Without morals a republic cannot subsist any length of time; they therefore who are decrying the Christian religion, whose morality is so sublime and pure . . . are undermining the solid foundation of morals, the best security for the duration of free governments.

CHARLES CARROLL | *signer of the Declaration of Independence*

WE RECOGNIZE NO
SOVEREIGN BUT GOD, AND
NO KING BUT JESUS!
JOHN HANCOCK *and* JOHN ADAMS

JOHN HANCOCK

With malice toward none, with charity for all, with
firmness in the right as God gives us to see the right, let
us strive . . . to bind up the nation's wounds . . . to do all
which may achieve and cherish a just and lasting peace
among ourselves and with all nations.
ABRAHAM LINCOLN | *March 4, 1865*

The general principles upon which the Fathers achieved
independence were the general principles of Christianity. . . .
Those general principles of Christianity are as eternal and
immutable as the existence and attributes of God.
JOHN ADAMS | *Second President*

117

The first permanent settlement in the New World was the English colony established in 1607 at Jamestown, Virginia. Similar to the other colonial charters, the First Charter of Virginia emphasized the Christian character of the colonists' purpose:

> We, greatly commending, and graciously accepting of, their desires for the furtherance of so noble a work, which may, by the providence of Almighty God, hereafter tend to the glory of His Divine Majesty, in propagating of Christian religion to such people, as yet live in darkness and miserable ignorance of the true knowledge and worship of God.

Similarly, in 1620, the Pilgrims established a colony at Plymouth, Massachusetts. Their purpose was to establish a political commonwealth governed by biblical standards. The Mayflower Compact, their initial governing document, clearly stated that what they had undertaken was for "the glory of God and the advancement of the Christian faith." William Bradford, the second governor of Plymouth, said, "[The colonists] cherished a great hope and inward zeal of laying good foundations . . . for the propagations and advance of the Gospel of the kingdom of Christ in the remote parts of the world."

"Go therefore and make disciples of all the nations, baptizing them in the name of the Father and of the Son and of the Holy Spirit, teaching them to observe all things that I have commanded you; and lo, I am with you always, even to the end of the age." Amen.

MATTHEW 28:19–20

★ ★ ★ ★

For I am not ashamed of the gospel of Christ, for it is the power of God to salvation for everyone who believes, for the Jew first and also for the Greek.

ROMANS 1:16

★ ★ ★ ★

Truly my soul silently waits for God;
   From Him comes my salvation.
He only is my rock and my salvation;
   He is my defense;
   I shall not be greatly moved.

PSALM 62:1–2

While several New Testament books confront the problem of false teachers, the short book of Jude goes beyond all other New Testament epistles in its passionate denunciation of the apostate teachers who have crept into the church. Combining the theme of 2 Peter with the style of James, Jude's letter is potent in spite of its brevity. Jude challenged believers—then and now—to contend for the faith and to expose anyone who was turning God's grace into unbounded license to do as they please. The danger was and is very real and not to be minimized.

Such vigilance is equally important when it comes to guarding our freedoms as Americans, and General Douglas MacArthur understood that. MacArthur officially accepted the Japanese surrender at the end of World War II, and when he oversaw the Occupation of Japan from 1945 to 1951, he was credited with implementing far-ranging democratic changes in that country. Well aware of the constant threats to freedom in this world, he stated, "No man is entitled to the blessings of freedom unless he be vigilant in its preservation."

*U.S. Army's First Division
Omaha Beach*

Finally, my brethren, be strong in the Lord and in the power of His might. Put on the whole armor of God, that you may be able to stand against the wiles of the devil. For we do not wrestle against flesh and blood, but against principalities, against powers, against the rulers of the darkness of this age, against spiritual hosts of wickedness in the heavenly places. Therefore take up the whole armor of God, that you may be able to withstand in the evil day, and having done all, to stand.

Stand therefore, having girded your waist with truth, having put on the breastplate of righteousness, and having shod your feet with the preparation of the gospel of peace; above all, taking the shield of faith with which you will be able to quench all the fiery darts of the wicked one. And take the helmet of salvation, and the sword of the Spirit, which is the word of God; praying always with all prayer and supplication in the Spirit, being watchful to this end with all perseverance and supplication for all the saints.

EPHESIANS 6:10–18

The book of Revelation unveils our Lord Jesus Christ at His Second Coming, the future times, and the world to come. Penned by the apostle John during his exile on the island of Patmos, Revelation centers around visions and symbols of the resurrected Christ, who alone has the authority to judge the earth, remake it, and rule it in righteousness. Revelation shows the divine plan of redemption being brought to fruition.

In the final chapter, Jesus Christ says to the apostle John, "I am the Alpha and the Omega, the Beginning and the End, the First and the Last" (22:13). There is no doubt that the risen Christ is indeed worthy to be praised and worshiped throughout eternity. It is interesting that in our nation's capital, the first and last rays of sunlight fall every day upon its tallest building—the 555-foot Washington Monument. And there on its top, inscribed on the four-sided aluminum capstone, are the Latin words *Laus Deo*, which means "Praise be to God." This simple expression of praise reflects America's abiding belief that God has blessed our country with liberty and divine favor.

Washington Monument

"I am He who lives, and was dead, and behold, I am alive forevermore. Amen. And I have the keys of Hades and of Death. Write the things which you have seen, and the things which are, and the things which will take place after this."

REVELATION 1:18–19

★ ★ ★ ★

"Behold, I stand at the door and knock. If anyone hears My voice and opens the door, I will come in to him and dine with him, and he with Me. To him who overcomes I will grant to sit with Me on My throne, as I also overcame and sat down with My Father on His throne."

REVELATION 3:20–21

★ ★ ★ ★

Blessed are those who do His commandments, that they may have the right to the tree of life, and may enter through the gates into the city.

REVELATION 22:14

In his 1801 inaugural address, President Thomas Jefferson (1743–1826) said the following:

Enlightened by a benign religion, professed, indeed, and practiced in various forms, yet all of them inculcating honesty, truth, temperance, gratitude, and the love of man; acknowledging and adoring an overruling Providence, which by all its dispensations proves that it delights in the happiness of man here and his greater happiness hereafter. With all these blessings, what more is necessary to make us a happy and prosperous people? Still one thing more, fellow citizens—a wise and frugal government, which shall restrain men from injuring one another, shall leave them otherwise free to regulate their own pursuits of industry and improvement, and shall not take from the mouth of labor the bread it has earned. . . .

You should understand what I deem the essential principles of our government. . . . Equal and exact justice to all men, of whatever state or persuasion, religious or political . . . the arraignment of all abuses at the bar of the public reason; freedom of religion.

Thomas Jefferson

He has shown you, O man, what is good;
And what does the LORD require of you
But to do justly,
To love mercy,
And to walk humbly with your God?

MICAH 6:8

★ ★ ★ ★

But those who desire to be rich fall into temptation and a snare, and into many foolish and harmful lusts which drown men in destruction and perdition. For the love of money is a root of all kinds of evil, for which some have strayed from the faith in their greediness, and pierced themselves through with many sorrows.

1 TIMOTHY 6:9–10

★ ★ ★ ★

For I, the LORD, love justice;
I hate robbery for burnt offering;
I will direct their work in truth,
And will make with them an everlasting covenant.

ISAIAH 61:8

In the 1844 *Vidal v. Girard's Executors*, Justice Joseph Story upheld the use of the Bible and the teaching of Christian moral principles in a city-run school.

In this case, Girard's will permitted the teaching of the Christian religion, just not by members of the clergy. Story's opinion that Girard's will was not derogatory to the Christian religion rested on two determinations. First, a layman was capable of teaching the general principles of Christianity: "Why may not laymen instruct in the general principles of Christianity as well as ecclesiastics?"

Second, Girard's will actually permitted the teaching of the Bible in the school:

> Why may not the Bible, and especially the New Testament, without note or comment be read and taught as a divine revelation ... its general precepts expounded, its evidences explained, and its glorious principles of morality inculcated? ... Where can the purest principles of morality be learned so clearly or so perfectly as from the New Testament? Where are benevolence, the love of truth, sobriety, and industry, so powerfully and irresistibly inculcated as in the sacred volume?

Joseph Story

126

Smoke went up from His nostrils,
   And devouring fire from His mouth;
   Coals were kindled by it.
He bowed the heavens also, and came down
   With darkness under His feet.
And He rode upon a cherub, and flew;
   He flew upon the wings of the wind.

PSALM 18:8–10

* * * *

My son, keep your father's command,
And do not forsake the law of your mother.
Bind them continually upon your heart;
Tie them around your neck.
When you roam, they will lead you;
When you sleep, they will keep you;
And when you awake, they will speak with you.
For the commandment is a lamp,
And the law a light;
Reproofs of instruction are the way of life.

PROVERBS 6:20–23

S imon Greenleaf (1783–1853) was the Royall
Professor of Law at Harvard and is considered one
of the greatest legal minds in Western history. Greenleaf
examined the evidence for the Resurrection, came to the
conclusion that it happened, and became a believer. In
his *Testimony of the Evangelists*, Greenleaf wrote:

> The religion of Jesus Christ aims at nothing less
> than the utter overthrow of all other systems
> of religion in the world; denouncing them as
> inadequate to the wants of man, false in their
> foundations, and dangerous in their tendency.
>
> These are no ordinary claims; and it seems hardly
> possible for a rational being to regard them with
> even a subdued interest; much less to treat them
> with mere indifference and contempt. If not true,
> they are little else than the pretensions of a bold
> imposture, which, not satisfied with having already
> enslaved millions of the human race, seeks to
> continue its encroachments upon human liberty, until
> all nations shall be subjugated under its iron rule.
>
> But if they are well-founded and just, they
> can be no less than the high requirements of
> heaven.

Simon Greenleaf

"Indeed the hour is coming, yes, has now come, that you will be scattered, each to his own, and will leave Me alone. And yet I am not alone, because the Father is with Me. These things I have spoken to you, that in Me you may have peace. In the world you will have tribulation; but be of good cheer, I have overcome the world."

JOHN 16:32–33

★ ★ ★ ★

"If you abide in Me, and My words abide in you, you will ask what you desire, and it shall be done for you. By this My Father is glorified, that you bear much fruit; so you will be My disciples."

JOHN 15:7–8

★ ★ ★ ★

"Let not your heart be troubled; you believe in God, believe also in Me. In My Father's house are many mansions; if it were not so, I would have told you. I go to prepare a place for you. And if I go and prepare a place for you, I will come again and receive you to Myself; that where I am, there you may be also."

JOHN 14:1–3

H ear these thoughts from Charles Malik (1906–1987), Lebanon's ambassador to the United Nations and president of the thirteenth session of the UN General Assembly in 1959:

> The good [in the United States] would never have come into being without the blessing and power of Jesus Christ. . . . Whoever tries to conceive the American word without taking full account of the suffering and love and salvation of Christ is only dreaming. I know how embarrassing this matter is to politicians, bureaucrats, businessmen, and cynics; but, whatever these honored men think, the irrefutable truth is that the soul of America is, at its best and highest, Christian.

Blessed is the nation whose God is the LORD,
    The people He has chosen as His own inheritance.
The LORD looks from heaven;
    He sees all the sons of men.
From the place of His dwelling He looks
    On all the inhabitants of the earth;
He fashions their hearts individually;
    He considers all their works.

PSALM 33:12–15

* * * *

For I am not ashamed of the gospel of Christ, for it is
the power of God to salvation for everyone who believes,
for the Jew first and also for the Greek. For in it the
righteousness of God is revealed from faith to faith; as it
is written, "The just shall live by faith."

ROMANS 1:16–17

After receiving Paul's first letter, the Corinthian church was swayed by false teachers who accused Paul of being proud, unimpressive, and unqualified to be an apostle of Jesus Christ. Recognizing this as spiritual war, Paul sent Titus to Corinth to address this issue.

Every believer needs to know that the opposition that comes their way has its source in evil forces that oppose God and His truth. As Paul himself wrote, "We do not wrestle against flesh and blood, but against principalities, against powers, against the rulers of the darkness of this age, against spiritual hosts of wickedness in the heavenly places" (Ephesians 6:12).

Whether they face immorality or false teaching, church leaders must take action to remedy the problem. The same is true of government. President Thomas Jefferson stated, "When once a republic is corrupted, there is no possibility of remedying any of the growing evils but by removing the corruption and restoring its lost principles; every other correction is either useless or a new evil."

For though we walk in the flesh, we do not war according to the flesh. For the weapons of our warfare are not carnal but mighty in God for pulling down strongholds, casting down arguments and every high thing that exalts itself against the knowledge of God, bringing every thought into captivity to the obedience of Christ.

2 CORINTHIANS 10:3–5

★ ★ ★ ★

Finally, my brethren, be strong in the Lord and in the power of His might. Put on the whole armor of God, that you may be able to stand against the wiles of the devil. For we do not wrestle against flesh and blood, but against principalities, against powers, against the rulers of the darkness of this age, against spiritual hosts of wickedness in the heavenly places.

EPHESIANS 6:10–12

★ ★ ★ ★

Therefore submit to God. Resist the devil and he will flee from you. Draw near to God and He will draw near to you. Cleanse your hands, you sinners; and purify your hearts, you double-minded.

JAMES 4:7–8

Jesus, Messiah and King

The Old Testament prophets predicted and longed for the coming of the Messiah, the One who would enter history to bring redemption and deliverance to God's chosen people. Through a carefully selected series of Old Testament quotations, the New Testament book of Matthew documents and verifies Jesus Christ's claim to be King of the Jews. In Matthew's gospel, Jesus' genealogy, baptism, messages, and miracles all clearly point to the same inescapable conclusion: Jesus is King, the long-awaited Messiah.

President Thomas Jefferson believed that the teachings of Jesus embody the "most sublime system of morals" in the whole world. He stated, "We all agree in the obligation of the moral precepts of Jesus, and nowhere will they be found delivered in greater purity than in His discourses."

Early in Jesus' public life, the apostle Peter recognized who this Carpenter was. In his gospel, Matthew confirmed that Jesus is the Messiah. And in his politics, Thomas Jefferson embraced His teachings. Who do you need to talk to about Jesus?

Thomas Jefferson

134

He is the image of the invisible God, the firstborn over all creation. For by Him all things were created that are in heaven and that are on earth, visible and invisible, whether thrones or dominions or principalities or powers. All things were created through Him and for Him.

COLOSSIANS 1:15–16

Then Jesus spoke to them again, saying, "I am the light of the world. He who follows Me shall not walk in darkness, but have the light of life."

JOHN 8:12

That you keep this commandment without spot, blameless until our Lord Jesus Christ's appearing, which He will manifest in His own time, He who is the blessed and only Potentate, the King of kings and Lord of lords, who alone has immortality, dwelling in unapproachable light, whom no man has seen or can see, to whom be honor and everlasting power. Amen.

1 TIMOTHY 6:14–16

Consider the boldness of Robert Winthrop, lawyer, philanthropist, and speaker of the U.S. House of Representatives:

> Men may as well build their houses upon the sand and expect to see them stand, when the rains fall, and the winds blow, and the floods come, as to found free institutions upon any other basis than that of morality and virtue, of which the Word of God is the only authoritative rule....
>
> All societies of men must be governed in some way or other. The less they have of stringent state government, the more they must have of individual self-government. The less they rely on public law or physical force, the more they must rely on private moral restraint.
>
> Men, in a word, must necessarily be controlled either by a power within them or a power without them; either by the Word of God or by the strong arm of man; either by the Bible or by the bayonet.
>
> It may do ... other governments to talk about the state supporting religion. Here, under our own free institutions, it is religion which must support the state.

Robert Winthrop

136

"Whoever hears these sayings of Mine, and does them, I will liken him to a wise man who built his house on the rock: and the rain descended, the floods came, and the winds blew and beat on that house; and it did not fall, for it was founded on the rock."

MATTHEW 7:24–25

★ ★ ★ ★

He shall judge between many peoples,
And rebuke strong nations afar off;
They shall beat their swords into plowshares,
And their spears into pruning hooks;
Nation shall not lift up sword against nation,
Neither shall they learn war anymore.
But everyone shall sit under his vine and under his fig tree,
And no one shall make them afraid;
For the mouth of the LORD of hosts has spoken.

MICAH 4:3–4

In 1775, Lutheran pastor John Peter Gabriel Muhlenberg concluded a sermon: "In the language of the Holy Writ, there is a time for all things. There is a time to preach and a time to fight. And now is the time to fight." He then threw off his clerical robes to reveal the uniform of a Revolutionary Army officer. That afternoon, at the head of three hundred men, he marched off to join General Washington's troops and became colonel of the 8th Virginia Regiment.

Ministers turned the colonial resistance into a righteous cause not only from the pulpit, but also in state legislatures and on the battlefield from military chaplains to taking up arms and leading troops into battle.

Ultimately, the Continental Army captured two key British armies at Saratoga in 1777 and Yorktown in 1781. That is when the prophetic words of Patrick Henry: "Three millions of people, armed with the holy cause of liberty, and in such a country as that which we possess, are invincible by any force which our enemy can send against us."

138

To everything there is a season,
    A time for every purpose under heaven. . . .
    A time to kill,
And a time to heal;
    A time to break down,
And a time to build up, . . .
    A time to love,
And a time to hate;
    A time of war,
And a time of peace.

ECCLESIASTES 3:1, 3, 8

★ ★ ★ ★

There is no fear in love; but perfect love casts out fear, because fear involves torment. But he who fears has not been made perfect in love. We love Him because He first loved us.

1 JOHN 4:18–19

Foundations are crucial to the success of any venture, whether it is building a house or building a nation. When the Founding Fathers set about to establish the bedrock that would define America's greatness, they went right to the source, declaring that all human beings are "endowed by their Creator with certain unalienable Rights."

The Bible contains the foundational truth that God is the Source of all life, sovereign over history, and our only hope for the peace, happiness, and true liberty we all crave. In Genesis, the "book of beginnings," we witness God's creation of heaven and earth by His powerful word, the beginnings of man's rebellion and sin, and God's calling of a covenant people through which He would bring salvation to all the peoples of the earth through His one and only Son.

I will make you a great nation;
    I will bless you
    And make your name great;
    And you shall be a blessing.
I will bless those who bless you,
    And I will curse him who curses you;
    And in you all the families of the earth shall
        be blessed.

GENESIS 12:2–3

* * * *

In Him also we have obtained an inheritance, being
predestined according to the purpose of Him who works
all things according to the counsel of His will, that we who
first trusted in Christ should be to the praise of His glory.

EPHESIANS 1:11–12

* * * *

The counsel of the LORD stands forever,
    The plans of His heart to all generations.
Blessed is the nation whose God is the LORD,
    The people He has chosen as His own inheritance.

PSALM 33:11–12

The founding of our beloved nation and the growth of Christ's glorious church share some inspiring parallels. Consider that America's Founders gathered at Independence Hall on July 4, 1776, to establish a nation that would be a beacon of hope and freedom to countless millions throughout the generations. Similarly, Christ's disciples gathered in Jerusalem to establish a church destined to take the hope of the gospel to the ends of the earth. Acts recounts the bold steps of faith the apostles took after they were filled with the power of the Holy Spirit. God used them to establish an ever-growing community of believers that models Christian virtue and faith in this dark, sin-filled world.

Just as America's Founding Fathers did, those early Christians faced many challenges, real dangers, and much opposition. But by God's grace as well as with prayer, hard work, and a steadfast reliance on the Almighty, they took the truth of the gospel to Jerusalem, Judea, Samaria, and the ends of the earth. Even today, the gospel of Jesus is the only hope for peace upon which individuals—or nations—can rely.

"You are My witnesses," says the Lord,
"And My servant whom I have chosen,
That you may know and believe Me,
And understand that I am He.
Before Me there was no God formed,
Nor shall there be after Me.
I, even I, am the Lord,
And besides Me there is no savior."

Isaiah 43:10–11

★ ★ ★ ★

"But you shall receive power when the Holy Spirit has come upon you; and you shall be witnesses to Me in Jerusalem, and in all Judea and Samaria, and to the end of the earth."

Acts 1:8

★ ★ ★ ★

"If anyone thirsts, let him come to Me and drink. He who believes in Me, as the Scripture has said, out of his heart will flow rivers of living water."

John 7:37–38

According to popular legend, John Hancock signed his name largely and distinctly to the Declaration of Independence so King George could read it without spectacles. While that may not be true, it is true that Mr. Hancock put his life on the line with that signature.

Each of the fifty-six signers knew the risk: "With a firm reliance on the protection of Divine Providence, we mutually pledge to each other our lives, our fortunes, and our sacred honor."

A few months before signing the Declaration, Patrick Henry addressed the Virginia Convention:

> We are not weak if we make a proper use of those means which the God of nature hath placed in our power. . . . Besides, sir, we shall not fight our battles alone. There is a just God who presides over the destinies of nations, and who will raise up friends to fight our battles for us.

Yet in the early 1990s, the authors of *The Day America Told the Truth* polled Americans about which beliefs they would die for—48 percent said "none." Only 30 percent would die for God, and fewer would die for their country.

John Hancock

144

★
★ ★

"This is My commandment, that you love one another as I have loved you. Greater love has no one than this, than to lay down one's life for his friends."

JOHN 15:12–13

★ ★ ★ ★

For to me, to live is Christ, and to die is gain. But if I live on in the flesh, this will mean fruit from my labor; yet what I shall choose I cannot tell.

PHILIPPIANS 1:21–22

★ ★ ★ ★

I beseech you therefore, brethren, by the mercies of God, that you present your bodies a living sacrifice, holy, acceptable to God, which is your reasonable service. And do not be conformed to this world, but be transformed by the renewing of your mind, that you may prove what is that good and acceptable and perfect will of God.

ROMANS 12:1–2

When Jonathan Edwards began preaching in Northampton, Massachusetts, in 1734, the moral conditions of that colony and throughout the British settlements were at an extreme low. The New England that was to be a "city on the hill" had become materialistic, the strict Puritan teachings no longer followed.

From the pulpit, Edwards stressed the importance of an immediate, personal spiritual rebirth. He preached the unworthiness of sinful man and the grace of God upon which any of us is totally dependent for salvation—and a revival began in his church, first among the youth and then spreading to the adults.

Edwards wrote that "in the spring and summer following, anno 1735, the town seemed to be so full of the presence of God; it never was so full of love, nor of joy, and yet so full of distress, as it was then." In two years, three hundred converts were added to the church, and news of the revival spread throughout New England.

Jonathan Edwards

"For God so loved the world that He gave His only begotten Son, that whoever believes in Him should not perish but have everlasting life. For God did not send His Son into the world to condemn the world, but that the world through Him might be saved."

JOHN 3:16–17

★ ★ ★ ★

That if you confess with your mouth the Lord Jesus and believe in your heart that God has raised Him from the dead, you will be saved. For with the heart one believes unto righteousness, and with the mouth confession is made unto salvation.

ROMANS 10:9–10

★ ★ ★ ★

For by grace you have been saved through faith, and that not of yourselves; it is the gift of God.

EPHESIANS 2:8

Medic Desmond Doss entered the U.S. Army in April 1942 as a conscientious objector because of his religious beliefs. From the beginning, men in his company harassed Doss for his faith. . . .

On Okinawa, in late spring of 1945, his battalion assaulted a jagged escarpment four hundred feet high— only to be met with artillery, mortar, and machine-gun fire that inflicted approximately seventy-five casualties. Doss remained with the many stricken, carrying them one by one to the edge of the cliff and lowering them down its face. Each time he prayed, "Dear God, let me get just one more man."

In three more battles in May, Doss unhesitatingly braved enemy artillery, mortar shells, and grenades to dress his fellow soldiers' wounds and evacuate them to safety. On May 21, he was seriously wounded when a grenade exploded. He waited five hours before litter bearers reached him. . . .

Discovering he had lost his Bible, Doss asked the men to watch for it. An entire battalion combed the battlefield, found the Bible, and mailed it to Doss.

Private First Class Doss became the first conscientious objector to receive the Medal of Honor for bravery.

Desmond Doss

The wicked flee when no one pursues,
But the righteous are bold as a lion.

PROVERBS 28:1

* * * *

Praying always with all prayer and supplication in the Spirit, being watchful to this end with all perseverance and supplication for all the saints—and for me, that utterance may be given to me, that I may open my mouth boldly to make known the mystery of the gospel.

EPHESIANS 6:18–19

* * * *

Let your conduct be without covetousness; be content with such things as you have. For He Himself has said, "I will never leave you nor forsake you." So we may boldly say:
"The LORD is my helper;
I will not fear.
What can man do to me?"

HEBREWS 13:5–6

D r. Luke penned the gospel that bears his name with the compassion of a family physician, carefully documenting the perfect humanity of Jesus Christ. Luke built this gospel narrative on the foundation of historical reliability, emphasizing Jesus' ancestry, birth, and early life before moving chronologically through His earthly ministry. Growing belief and growing opposition developed side by side, with the opposition finally sending the Son of Man to His death on the cross. But Jesus' resurrection ensured that His purpose of saving the lost was fulfilled.

Christianity welcomes close examination, that the inquirer might "know the certainty" of its truths (Luke 1:4). Alexander Hamilton, a signer of the Constitution and one of America's first constitutional lawyers, made such an investigation. This is his conclusion: "I have carefully examined the evidences of the Christian religion, and if I was sitting as a juror upon its authenticity, I would unhesitatingly give my verdict in its favor. I can prove its truth as clearly as any proposition ever submitted to the mind of man."

Alexander Hamilton

150

Then Jesus said to them, "When you lift up the Son of Man, then you will know that I am He, and that I do nothing of Myself; but as My Father taught Me, I speak these things. And He who sent Me is with Me. The Father has not left Me alone, for I always do those things that please Him."

JOHN 8:28–29

★ ★ ★ ★

"Most assuredly, I say to you, the hour is coming, and now is, when the dead will hear the voice of the Son of God; and those who hear will live. For as the Father has life in Himself, so He has granted the Son to have life in Himself."

JOHN 5:25–26

★ ★ ★ ★

"For the Son of Man has come to seek and to save that which was lost."

LUKE 19:10

Paul, the aged and experienced apostle, wrote to the young pastor Timothy, who was facing a heavy burden of responsibility in the church at Ephesus. False teachings needed to be corrected; public worship, safeguarded; and mature leadership, developed. Paul spoke pointedly about a minister's proper conduct and counseled Timothy on the qualities that make for a godly leader. A Christ-follower must be careful to avoid false teachers and greedy motives, pursuing instead righteousness, godliness, faith, love, perseverance, and the gentleness that befit a servant of God.

As he took over responsibility for the church Paul founded at Ephesus, Timothy could not be a second Paul, but he would need to use all his God-given strengths to lead the church. Likewise, American writer and humorist Charles F. Browne said, "We can't all be Washingtons, but we can all be patriots." We will never be the father of our country, but we can serve our country to the best of our abilities.

For you, brethren, have been called to liberty; only do not use liberty as an opportunity for the flesh, but through love serve one another.

GALATIANS 5:13

★ ★ ★ ★

For if the blood of bulls and goats and the ashes of a heifer, sprinkling the unclean, sanctifies for the purifying of the flesh, how much more shall the blood of Christ, who through the eternal Spirit offered Himself without spot to God, cleanse your conscience from dead works to serve the living God?

HEBREWS 9:13–14

★ ★ ★ ★

Serve the LORD with gladness;
    Come before His presence with singing.
Know that the LORD, He is God;
    It is He who has made us, and not we ourselves;
    We are His people and the sheep of His pasture.

PSALM 100:2–3

"God of Our Fathers"

C ivil War veteran and rector of a small
Episcopal parish in Brandon, Vermont,
Daniel C. Roberts wanted a new hymn for
his congregation to sing in celebration of
the American Centennial in 1876. He wrote
"God of Our Fathers," and his congregation
sang it on July 4. In 1892, this hymn was
chosen to be sung at the centennial
celebration of the United States Constitution.

Daniel C. Roberts

God of our fathers, whose almighty hand
   Leads forth in beauty all the starry band
   Of shining worlds in splendor through the skies
   Our grateful songs before Thy throne arise.

Thy love divine hath led us in the past,
   In this free land by Thee our lot is cast,
   Be Thou our Ruler, Guardian, Guide, and Stay,
   Thy Word our law, Thy paths our chosen way.

From war's alarms, from deadly pestilence,
   Be Thy strong arm our ever sure defense;
   Thy true religion in our hearts increase,
   Thy bounteous goodness nourish us in peace.

Refresh Thy people on their toilsome way,
   Lead us from night to never ending day;
   Fill all our lives with love and grace divine,
   And glory, laud, and praise be ever Thine.

In 1984, University of Houston political scientists Donald Lutz and Charles Hyneman wrote about the sources that most influenced the development of American political thought during our nation's Founding Era, 1760–1805. "The Relative Influence of European Writers on Late Eighteenth-Century American Political Thought" was published in *The American Political Science Review*, 78 (1984).

After analyzing some fifteen thousand items published during that forty-five-year period, the authors isolated 3,154 direct quotes cited by the Founders . . . and discovered that 34 percent came directly out of the Bible. French legal philosopher Baron Charles de Montesquieu was quoted 8.3 percent of the time. Sir William Blackstone, a renowned English jurist whose *Commentaries on the Laws of England* were highly accepted in America, was next at 7.9 percent, and English philosopher John Locke was fourth with 2.9 percent.

Three-fourths of the biblical citations . . . came from reprinted sermons, and only 9 percent came from secular literature. These statistics clearly reflect the Bible's impact on the Founding Fathers.

As for God, His way is perfect;
    The word of the LORD is proven;
    He is a shield to all who trust in Him.
For who is God, except the LORD?
    And who is a rock, except our God?

PSALM 18:30–31

* * * *

For the word of God is living and powerful, and sharper than any two-edged sword, piercing even to the division of soul and spirit, and of joints and marrow, and is a discerner of the thoughts and intents of the heart.

HEBREWS 4:12

* * * *

So shall My word be that goes forth from My mouth;
It shall not return to Me void,
But it shall accomplish what I please,
And it shall prosper in the thing for which I sent it.

ISAIAH 55:11

Ronald Reagan, the fortieth president of the United States (1981–1989), wrote the following:

The family has always been the cornerstone of American society. Our families nurture, preserve, and pass on to each succeeding generation the values we share and cherish, values that are the foundation for our freedoms. In the family, we learn our first lessons of God and man, love and discipline, rights and responsibilities, human dignity and human frailty.

Our families give us daily examples of these lessons being put into practice. In raising and instructing our children, in providing personal and compassionate care for the elderly, in maintaining the spiritual strength of religious commitment among our people—in these and other ways, America's families make immeasurable contributions to America's well-being.

Today more than ever, it is essential that these contributions not be taken for granted and that each of us remember that the strength of our families is vital to the strength of our nation.

Ronald and Nancy Reagan and family

God sets the solitary in families;
He brings out those who are bound into prosperity.

PSALM 68:6

* * * *

Honor your father and your mother, that your days may be long upon the land which the LORD your God is giving you.

EXODUS 20:12

* * * *

Now, therefore, you are no longer strangers and foreigners, but fellow citizens with the saints and members of the household of God, having been built on the foundation of the apostles and prophets, Jesus Christ Himself being the chief cornerstone, in whom the whole building, being fitted together, grows into a holy temple in the Lord, in whom you also are being built together for a dwelling place of God in the Spirit.

EPHESIANS 2:19–22

As the president of Yale College, Ezra Stiles spoke before the governor and the General Assembly of Connecticut in May 1783:

> In our lowest and most dangerous state . . . we sustained ourselves against the British Army of sixty thousand troops, commanded by . . . the ablest generals Britain could procure . . . with a naval force of twenty-two thousand seamen. . . .
>
> Who but a Washington, inspired by Heaven, could have conceived the surprise move upon the enemy at Princeton—that Christmas eve when Washington and his army crossed the Delaware?
>
> Who but the Ruler of the winds could have delayed the British reinforcements by three months of contrary ocean winds at a critical point of the war?
>
> Or what but "a providential miracle" at the last minute detected the treacherous scheme of traitor Benedict Arnold, which would have delivered the American army . . . into the hands of the enemy?
>
> On the French role in the Revolution, it is God who so ordered the balancing interests of nations. . . .
>
> The United States are under peculiar obligations to become a holy people unto the Lord our God.

Ezra Stiles

160

God has spoken once,
  Twice I have heard this:
  That power belongs to God.
Also to You, O Lord, belongs mercy;
  For You render to each one according to his work.

PSALM 62:11–12

* * * *

For the Scripture says to the Pharaoh, "For this very purpose I have raised you up, that I may show My power in you, and that My name may be declared in all the earth." Therefore He has mercy on whom He wills, and whom He wills He hardens.

ROMANS 9:17–18

* * * *

For the message of the cross is foolishness to those who are perishing, but to us who are being saved it is the power of God.

1 CORINTHIANS 1:18

In his May 12, 1962, farewell speech to the Corps of Cadets at West Point, General Douglas MacArthur gave a moving tribute to the American soldier. The following paragraph is from that stirring speech:

Duty, Honor, Country. . . .

The code which those words perpetuate embraces the highest moral laws and will stand the test of any ethics or philosophies ever promulgated for the uplift of mankind. Its requirements are for the things that are right, and its restraints are from the things that are wrong. The soldier, above all other men, is required to practice the greatest act of religious training—sacrifice. In battle and in the face of danger and death, he discloses those divine attributes which his Maker gave when He created man in His own image. No physical courage and no brute instinct can take the place of the Divine help which alone can sustain [the soldier]. However horrible the incidents of war may be, the soldier who is called upon to offer and to give his life for his country is the noblest development of mankind.

Douglas MacArthur

The LORD is my rock and my fortress and my deliverer;
    My God, my strength, in whom I will trust;
My shield and the horn of my salvation, my
       stronghold.

PSALM 18:2

* * * *

Honor and majesty are before Him;
    Strength and beauty are in His sanctuary.
Give to the LORD, O families of the peoples,
    Give to the LORD glory and strength.
Give to the LORD the glory due His name.

PSALM 96:6–8

* * * *

For this is the will of God, that by doing good you may
put to silence the ignorance of foolish men—as free, yet
not using liberty as a cloak for vice, but as bondservants
of God. Honor all people. Love the brotherhood. Fear
God. Honor the king.

1 PETER 2:15–17

According to Margaret Truman, the most difficult decision Harry S. Truman faced as president was whether to support the creation of a Jewish homeland in Palestine after World War II. "I am trying to . . . make the whole world safe for Jews," he wrote. In November 1947, he lobbied for the United Nations' resolution that divided Palestine into Jewish and Arab states.

Great Britain announced it would transfer its authority over Palestine to the United Nations by May 14, 1948. On the eve of British withdrawal, most American experts strongly opposed the creation of a Jewish state, warning Truman that Arab countries would cut off oil and unite to destroy the Jews. But Truman weighed the multifaceted concerns and held firm.

The nation's first prime minister, David Ben-Gurion, read a declaration of Jewish independence: "The name of our state shall be Israel." At midnight, British rule over Palestine lapsed; eleven minutes later, White House spokesman Charlie Ross announced U.S. recognition.

The American statement recognizing the new State of Israel bears President Truman's last-minute handwritten changes.

With Truman's decision, the hopes of the Jewish people were realized.

Harry S. Truman

The LORD builds up Jerusalem;
    He gathers together the outcasts of Israel.
He heals the brokenhearted
    And binds up their wounds.

PSALM 147:2–3

If I forget you, O Jerusalem,
    Let my right hand forget its skill!
If I do not remember you,
    Let my tongue cling to the roof of my mouth—
    If I do not exalt Jerusalem
    Above my chief joy.

PSALM 137:5–6

Pray for the peace of Jerusalem:
    "May they prosper who love you.
Peace be within your walls,
    Prosperity within your palaces."
For the sake of my brethren and companions,
    I will now say, "Peace be within you."

PSALM 122:6–8

Genuinely Good Works

F ounding Father Benjamin Franklin wrote the
following:

I can only show my gratitude for these mercies
from God, by a readiness to help His other children
and my brethren. For I do not think that thanks
and compliments, though repeated weekly, can
discharge our real obligations to each other, and
much less those to our Creator.

The faith you mention has certainly its use in
the world. . . . But I wish it were more productive
of good works than I have generally seen it; I mean
real good works; works of kindness, charity, mercy,
and public spirit; not holiday keeping, sermon
reading or hearing; performing church ceremonies,
or making long prayers, filled with flatteries and
compliments. . . .

The worship of God is a duty; the hearing
and reading of sermons may be useful;
but, if men rest in hearing and praying,
as too many do, it is as if a tree
should value itself on being watered
and putting forth leaves, though it
never produce any fruit.

Benjamin Franklin

166

For we are His workmanship, created in Christ Jesus for good works, which God prepared beforehand that we should walk in them.

EPHESIANS 2:10

* * * *

But in a great house there are not only vessels of gold and silver, but also of wood and clay, some for honor and some for dishonor. Therefore if anyone cleanses himself from the latter, he will be a vessel for honor, sanctified and useful for the Master, prepared for every good work.

2 TIMOTHY 2:20–21

* * * *

"Either make the tree good and its fruit good, or else make the tree bad and its fruit bad; for a tree is known by its fruit. . . . A good man out of the good treasure of his heart brings forth good things, and an evil man out of the evil treasure brings forth evil things. . . . For by your words you will be justified, and by your words you will be condemned."

MATTHEW 12:33, 35, 37

God's Bigger Shovel

Frustrated at his first job—moving dirt by hand—R. G. LeTourneau (1888–1969) was committed to finding a better, more efficient way to get the work done. As the father of the modern earthmoving industry, he is credited with nearly three hundred inventions, including the bulldozer, scrapers of all sorts, dredgers, portable cranes, . . . and many others. During World War II, he produced 70 percent of all the army's earthmoving machinery.

With Matthew 6:33 as his life verse, LeTourneau felt called to be a "businessman for God," saying that God was the Chairman of his board. He established the LeTourneau Foundation to channel 90 percent of his multimillion-dollar salary to Christian endeavors. LeTourneau was convinced that he could not outgive God: "I shovel it out, and God shovels it back, but God has a bigger shovel."

LeTourneau's business efforts never deterred him from his reason for existence: to glorify God and spread the gospel. He shared his faith with millions, founded missionary efforts in Liberia and Peru, and, with his wife, founded a college in Longview, Texas. LeTourneau University has produced more than ten thousand alumni who are faithfully serving the Lord in all fifty states and in fifty-five nations.

R. G. LeTourneau

168

For he who sows to his flesh will of the flesh reap corruption, but he who sows to the Spirit will of the Spirit reap everlasting life. And let us not grow weary while doing good, for in due season we shall reap if we do not lose heart.

GALATIANS 6:8–9

★ ★ ★ ★

"But seek first the kingdom of God and His righteousness, and all these things shall be added to you. Therefore do not worry about tomorrow, for tomorrow will worry about its own things. Sufficient for the day is its own trouble."

MATTHEW 6:33–34

★ ★ ★ ★

"Give, and it will be given to you: good measure, pressed down, shaken together, and running over will be put into your bosom. For with the same measure that you use, it will be measured back to you."

LUKE 6:38

A philanthropist later in life, Samuel Colgate (1822–1897) was the American manufacturer whose industriousness resulted in the Colgate-Palmolive Company. Clearly he recognized Jesus as God's Son and the value of the Word:

> The only spiritual light in the world comes through Jesus Christ and the inspired Book; redemption and forgiveness of sin alone through Christ. Without His presence and the teachings of the Bible, we would be enshrouded in moral darkness and despair.
>
> The condition of those nations without a Christ, contrasted with those where Christ is accepted, reveals so marked a difference that no arguments are needed. It is an object lesson so plain that it can be seen and understood by all. May "the earth be full of the knowledge of the Lord, as the waters cover the sea."

"Nor do they light a lamp and put it under a basket, but on a lampstand, and it gives light to all who are in the house. Let your light so shine before men, that they may see your good works and glorify your Father in heaven."

MATTHEW 5:15–16

* * * *

Then Jesus said to them, "A little while longer the light is with you. Walk while you have the light, lest darkness overtake you; he who walks in darkness does not know where he is going. While you have the light, believe in the light, that you may become sons of light."

JOHN 12:35–36

* * * *

For you were once darkness, but now you are light in the Lord. Walk as children of light (for the fruit of the Spirit is in all goodness, righteousness, and truth), finding out what is acceptable to the Lord.

EPHESIANS 5:8–10

After the Boston Tea Party, the British navy retaliated by blockading the port of Boston. The colonies surrounding Massachusetts responded with sympathy and action. On May 24, 1773, the House of Burgesses in Virginia proposed and approved a Day of Fasting, Humiliation, and Prayer:

> This House, being deeply impressed with apprehension of the great dangers to be derived to British America from the hostile invasion of the city of Boston . . . whose commerce and harbor are, on the first day of June next, to be stopped by an armed force, deem it highly necessary that the said first day of June be set apart . . . as a Day of Fasting, Humiliation, and Prayer; devoutly to implore the Divine interposition, for averting the heavy calamity which threatens destruction to our civil rights and the evils of civil war; to give us one heart and mind firmly opposed . . . [to] every injury to American rights; and that the minds of his Majesty and his Parliament, may be inspired from above with wisdom, moderation, and justice, to remove from the loyal people of America all cause of danger from a continued pursuit of measures pregnant with their ruin.

The Boston Tea Party

172

"Now, therefore," says the LORD,
"Turn to Me with all your heart,
With fasting, with weeping, and with mourning."
So rend your heart, and not your garments;
Return to the LORD your God,
For He is gracious and merciful,
Slow to anger, and of great kindness;
And He relents from doing harm.

JOEL 2:12–13

* * * *

"Because of your unbelief; for assuredly, I say to you,
if you have faith as a mustard seed, you will say to this
mountain, 'Move from here to there,' and it will move;
and nothing will be impossible for you. However, this
kind does not go out except by prayer and fasting."

MATTHEW 17:20–21

* * * *

"But you, when you fast, anoint your head and wash
your face, so that you do not appear to men to be
fasting, but to your Father who is in the secret place; and
your Father who sees in secret will reward you openly."

MATTHEW 6:17–18

The Declaration of Independence declared not only the colonies' independence from Britain, but also a dependence on "the Laws of Nature and of Nature's God." These had been defined by historic legal writers, such as Sir William Blackstone, as the laws that God had established for the governance of people, nations, and nature. Blackstone's *Commentaries on the Law*, the primary law book of the Founding Fathers, defined "the laws of nature" as the will of God for man.

> Man, considered as a creature, must necessarily be subject to the laws of his Creator, for he is entirely a dependent being. . . . It is necessary that he should in all points conform to his Maker's will. This will of his Maker is called the law of nature. . . . It is binding over all the globe, in all countries, and at all times; no human laws are of any validity, if contrary to this. . . .
>
> But every man now finds that his reason is corrupt, and his understanding full of ignorance and error. . . . The doctrines thus delivered we call the revealed or divine law, and they are to be found only in the Holy Scriptures. . . .
>
> Upon these two foundations . . . no human laws should be suffered to contradict these.

Sir William Blackstone

Only may the LORD give you wisdom and understanding, and give you charge concerning Israel, that you may keep the law of the LORD your God. Then you will prosper, if you take care to fulfill the statutes and judgments with which the LORD charged Moses concerning Israel. Be strong and of good courage; do not fear nor be dismayed.

1 CHRONICLES 22:12–13

Blessed is the man
    Who walks not in the counsel of the ungodly,
    Nor stands in the path of sinners,
    Nor sits in the seat of the scornful;
But his delight is in the law of the LORD,
    And in His law he meditates day and night.

PSALM 1:1–2

Blessed are the undefiled in the way,
    Who walk in the law of the LORD!
Blessed are those who keep His testimonies,
    Who seek Him with the whole heart!

PSALM 119:1–2

Noticing the migration west from the Appalachian cabins to settlements along the Oregon Trail, the American Sunday School Union (ASSU) set as a goal to establish a Sunday school in every new community on the western frontier and sent out a large number of missionaries to make that happen. These Sunday schools eventually gave rise to thousands of churches across America.

One example of the tremendous influence the Sunday school movement had in American frontier life was the Mississippi Valley Enterprise (MVE), the effort of the ASSU to "establish a Sunday school in every destitute place where it is practicable throughout the Valley of the Mississippi." In fifty years, the MVE established over 61,000 Sunday schools and enrolled 2,650,000 pupils. Remarkably, during his twenty years of service, missionary Stephen Paxson, who was born with a speech impediment that later earned him the nickname "Stuttering Stephen," started 1,314 Sunday schools that taught 83,000 students about Jesus' love for them.

So then faith comes by hearing, and hearing by the word of God.

ROMANS 10:17

* * * *

Listen carefully to Me, and eat what is good,
And let your soul delight itself in abundance.
Incline your ear, and come to Me.
Hear, and your soul shall live.

ISAIAH 55:2–3

* * * *

And you shall teach them the statutes and the laws, and show them the way in which they must walk and the work they must do.

EXODUS 18:20

* * * *

Teach me Your way, O LORD,
    And lead me in a smooth path.

PSALM 27:11

There is no better source of practical wisdom and instruction for how to live an upright and righteous life than the book of Proverbs. Its counsel, however, is not just relevant to individuals, but to nations as well. Proverbs 14:34, for instance, is a truth that godly leaders have cited for generations: "Righteousness exalts a nation, but sin is a reproach to any people."

Patrick Henry, one of early America's most outspoken Revolutionary leaders, predicted that whether or not the newly formed United States would prove "a blessing or a curse will depend upon the use our people make of the blessings which a gracious God hath bestowed on us. If they are wise, they will be great and happy. If they are of a contrary character, they will be miserable. Righteousness alone can exalt them as a nation."

The state of our nation today suggests we have strayed from God's wisdom. We—as individuals and corporately as a nation— must seek God and His righteousness if we are to continue in His grace.

Patrick Henry

178

Get wisdom! Get understanding!
Do not forget, nor turn away from the words of
      my mouth.
Do not forsake her, and she will preserve you;
Love her, and she will keep you.
Wisdom is the principal thing;
Therefore get wisdom.
And in all your getting, get understanding.

PROVERBS 4:5–7

He who heeds the word wisely will find good,
And whoever trusts in the LORD, happy is he.
The wise in heart will be called prudent,
And sweetness of the lips increases learning.

PROVERBS 16:20–21

On Memorial Day in 1923, Calvin Coolidge, the thirtieth president of the United States, spoke about the Puritan forefathers:

> If there be a destiny, it is of no avail to us unless we work with it. The ways of Providence will be of no advantage to us unless we proceed in the same direction. If we perceive a destiny in America, if we believe that Providence has been our guide, our own success, our own salvation requires that we should act and serve in harmony and obedience....
>
> Settlers came here from mixed motives, some for pillage and adventure, some for trade and refuge, but those who have set their imperishable mark upon our institutions came from far higher motives.... They were intent upon establishing a Christian commonwealth in accordance to the principle of self-government.
>
> They were an inspired body of men.... They had a genius for organized society on the foundations of piety, righteousness, liberty, and obedience of the law. They brought with them the accumulated wisdom and experience of the ages.... Who can fail to see ... the hand of destiny? Who can doubt that it has been guided by a Divine Providence?

Calvin Coolidge

Therefore be careful to observe them; for this is your wisdom and your understanding in the sight of the peoples who will hear all these statutes, and say, "Surely this great nation is a wise and understanding people."

DEUTERONOMY 4:6

* * * *

Bondservants, be obedient to those who are your masters according to the flesh, with fear and trembling, in sincerity of heart, as to Christ; not with eye service, as men-pleasers, but as bondservants of Christ, doing the will of God from the heart, with goodwill doing service, as to the Lord, and not to men, knowing that whatever good anyone does, he will receive the same from the Lord, whether he is a slave or free.

EPHESIANS 6:5–8

A s Americans moved West in the late 1700s, preachers braved cold weather, lack of roads, and threat of Indian attacks to take the gospel to the pioneers.

Led by the colossal efforts of Francis Asbury, who traveled nearly 300,000 miles on horseback and preached more than 16,000 sermons, an army of Methodist circuit riders was inspired to go wherever the pioneers went. In that span of time, the denomination grew in number from only 300 members with four ministers to over 200,000 members with 2,000 ministers, many of whom had little formal education. The Methodists also gave unprecedented freedom to both women and African-Americans.

Similarly, the Baptists sent out "farmer-preachers." Most of them had little education and were poorly paid, but they were in touch with the pioneers' lives. With an emphasis on the need for a personal conversion and salvation from sin through faith in Jesus Christ, these ministers spread the gospel far and wide. The Baptists made it easy for committed laypeople to be involved in God's kingdom work.

Francis Asbury

182

And He said to them, "Go into all the world and preach the gospel to every creature. He who believes and is baptized will be saved."

MARK 16:15–16

* * *

"The Spirit of the LORD is upon Me,
Because He has anointed Me
To preach the gospel to the poor;
He has sent Me to heal the brokenhearted,
To proclaim liberty to the captives
And recovery of sight to the blind,
To set at liberty those who are oppressed;
To proclaim the acceptable year of the LORD."

LUKE 4:18–19

* * *

I charge you therefore before God and the Lord Jesus Christ, who will judge the living and the dead at His appearing and His kingdom: Preach the word! Be ready in season and out of season. Convince, rebuke, exhort, with all longsuffering and teaching.

2 TIMOTHY 4:1–2

William Samuel Johnson (1727–1819), president of Columbia University (King's College before 1784), spoke to the first graduating class after the Revolutionary War:

> You have ... received a public education, the purpose whereof hath been to qualify you the better to serve your Creator and your country. ... Your first great duties ... are those you owe to Heaven, to your Creator and Redeemer. Let these be ever present to your minds and exemplified in your lives and conduct. ...
>
> The fear of God is the beginning of wisdom, and its consummation is everlasting felicity. ... Remember, too, that you are the redeemed of the Lord, that you are bought with a price, even the inestimable price of the precious blood of the Son of God. Adore Jehovah, therefore, as your God and your Judge. Love, fear, and serve Him as your Creator, Redeemer, and Sanctifier. Make Him your friend and protector and your felicity is secured both here and hereafter.

William Samuel Johnson

And now, Israel, what does the LORD your God require of you, but to fear the LORD your God, to walk in all His ways and to love Him, to serve the LORD your God with all your heart and with all your soul, and to keep the commandments of the LORD and His statutes which I command you today for your good?

DEUTERONOMY 10:12–13

★ ★ ★ ★

Trust in the LORD with all your heart,
And lean not on your own understanding;
In all your ways acknowledge Him,
And He shall direct your paths.

PROVERBS 3:5–6

★ ★ ★ ★

"Take My yoke upon you and learn from Me, for I am gentle and lowly in heart, and you will find rest for your souls. For My yoke is easy and My burden is light."

MATTHEW 11:29–30

The Key to Survival

On June 2, 1995, U.S. Air Force Captain Scott O'Grady was patrolling the United Nations designated no-fly zone over war-torn Bosnia when, at 27,000 feet, his F-16 fighter was struck by a surface-to-air missile. He desperately pulled his ejection lever and was catapulted into the sky at 350 miles per hour. Remarkably, he managed to land unscathed—but in enemy territory.

For six incredible days and nights, O'Grady eluded capture by the Bosnian Serbs who relentlessly pursued him. Relying in part on his military survival training, O'Grady said his faith in God also sustained him. During his third day on the ground, he experienced the love of God to such a degree that it took away his fear of death. On the sixth day, in a daring daylight rescue, an elite team of Marines moved in with a chopper, dodged enemy fire, and pulled the young American to safety.

At a national press conference following his triumphant return to the U.S., O'Grady said, "If it weren't for my love for God and God's love for me, I wouldn't be here right now."

Scott O'Grady

Wait on the LORD;
    Be of good courage,
    And He shall strengthen your heart;
    Wait, I say, on the LORD!

PSALM 27:14

★ ★ ★ ★

The LORD is my light and my salvation;
    Whom shall I fear?
    The LORD is the strength of my life;
    Of whom shall I be afraid?

PSALM 27:1

★ ★ ★ ★

He who dwells in the secret place of the Most High
    Shall abide under the shadow of the Almighty.
I will say of the LORD, "He is my refuge and my fortress;
    My God, in Him I will trust."

PSALM 91:1–2

In June 1630, John Winthrop landed in Massachusetts Bay with seven hundred people in eleven ships, thus beginning the Great Migration. During this sixteen-year period, more than 20,000 Puritans sailed for New England. The Puritans so believed that this New World would be free of the corruptions in their own church-state homeland, they called their colony a "Zion in wilderness" and "a city upon a hill." Winthrop stated that the aim of the colonists was "to advance the kingdom of our Lord Jesus Christ, and to enjoy the liberties of the gospel thereof in purities and peace."

In 1638, the Reverend John Davenport and Theophilus Eaton established a colony in New Haven, Connecticut. A year later, the Fundamental Orders of Connecticut was adopted.

> For as much as it hath pleased Almighty God by the wise disposition of His Divine Providence ... and well knowing where a people are gathered together the Word of God requires that to maintain the peace and union of such a people there should be an orderly and decent government established according to God, to order and dispose of the affairs of the people at all seasons as occasion shall require.

John Winthrop

188

"You are the light of the world. A city that is set on a hill cannot be hidden. Nor do they light a lamp and put it under a basket, but on a lampstand, and it gives light to all who are in the house. Let your light so shine before men, that they may see your good works and glorify your Father in heaven."

MATTHEW 5:14–16

＊ ＊ ＊ ＊

Then Jesus spoke to them again, saying, "I am the light of the world. He who follows Me shall not walk in darkness, but have the light of life."

JOHN 8:12

＊ ＊ ＊ ＊

This is the message which we have heard from Him and declare to you, that God is light and in Him is no darkness at all. If we say that we have fellowship with Him, and walk in darkness, we lie and do not practice the truth. But if we walk in the light as He is in the light, we have fellowship with one another, and the blood of Jesus Christ His Son cleanses us from all sin.

1 JOHN 1:5–7

A D-Day Prayer

President Franklin D. Roosevelt read this prayer, originally entitled "Let Our Hearts Be Stout," over radio to an anxious nation as Allied troops were invading Nazi-occupied Europe on D-Day, June 6, 1944:

> Almighty God, our sons, pride of our nation, this day have set upon a mighty endeavor, a struggle to preserve our Republic, our religion, and our civilization, and to set free a suffering humanity. Lead them straight and true; give strength to their arms, stoutness to their hearts, steadfastness in their faith.
>
> They will need Thy blessings. Their road will be long and hard. . . .
>
> [Our men] fight to liberate. They fight to let justice arise and tolerance and goodwill among all Thy people. They yearn but for the end of battle, for their return to the haven of home. Some will never return. Embrace these, Father, and receive them, Thy heroic servants, into Thy kingdom.
>
> With Thy blessing, we shall prevail over the unholy forces of our enemy. . . .
>
> Thy will be done, Almighty God. Amen.

U.S. Army's First Division
Omaha Beach

O LORD, God of my salvation,
I have cried out day and night before You.
Let my prayer come before You;
Incline Your ear to my cry.
For my soul is full of troubles.

PSALM 88:1–3

★ ★ ★ ★

The LORD will command His lovingkindness in
the daytime,
And in the night His song shall be with me—
A prayer to the God of my life.

PSALM 42:8

★ ★ ★ ★

Now therefore, our God, hear the prayer of Your servant,
and his supplications, and for the Lord's sake cause Your
face to shine on Your sanctuary, which is desolate.

DANIEL 9:17

Founder of the Hilton Hotel chain, Conrad Hilton (1887–1979) published this prayer on full-page ads in major magazines on July 4, 1952:

Our Father in heaven.

We pray that You save us from ourselves.

The world that You have made for us, to live in peace, we have made into an armed camp. We live in fear of war to come. We are afraid of "the terror that flies by night, and the arrow that flies by day, the pestilence that walks in darkness and the destruction that wastes at noon-day."

We have turned from You to go our selfish way. We have broken Your commandments and denied Your truth. We have left Your altars to serve the false gods of money and pleasure and power.

Forgive us and help us.

Now, darkness gathers around us, and we are confused in all our counsels. Losing faith in You, we lose faith in ourselves.

Be swift to save us, dear God, before the darkness falls.

192

But You, O LORD, are a shield for me,
My glory and the One who lifts up my head.

PSALM 3:3

* * * *

Let us hold fast the confession of our hope without wavering, for He who promised is faithful. And let us consider one another in order to stir up love and good works.

HEBREWS 10:23–24

* * * *

Get wisdom! Get understanding!
Do not forget, nor turn away from the words of
my mouth.
Do not forsake her, and she will preserve you;
Love her, and she will keep you.
Wisdom is the principal thing;
Therefore get wisdom.
And in all your getting, get understanding.

PROVERBS 4:5–7

"The Battle Hymn of the Republic"

Julia Ward Howe

I n November 1861, after visiting a Union Army camp, Julia Ward Howe wrote the poem that came to be called "The Battle Hymn of the Republic."

Mine eyes have seen the glory of the coming of the Lord:
He is trampling out the vintage where the grapes of
*   wrath are stored;*
He hath loosed the fateful lightning of His terrible
*   swift sword:*
His truth is marching on.

I have seen Him in the watch-fires of a hundred
         circling camps,
They have builded Him an altar in the evening dews
         and damps;
I can read His righteous sentence by the dim and
         flaring lamps:
His day is marching on.
I have read a fiery gospel writ in burnished rows of steel:
"As ye deal with my contemners, so with you my grace
         shall deal;
Let the Hero, born of woman, crush the serpent with
         His heel,
Since God is marching on."
He has sounded forth the trumpet that shall never
         call retreat;
He is sifting out the hearts of men before His
         judgment-seat:
Oh, be swift, my soul, to answer Him! be jubilant,
         my feet!
Our God is marching on.
In the beauty of the lilies Christ was born across the sea,
With a glory in His bosom that transfigures you and me:
As He died to make men holy, let us die to make
         men free,
While God is marching on.

Photo Credits

• 98©2008Jupiterimages Corporation • 100Sir Thomas HydePage • 102Anthony Berger • 104Sclchua (Wikimedia Commons) • 106Library of Congress • 108The Bay State Monthly, Volume I. No. VI. June, 1884 • 110Frances Benjamin Johnston • 112Courtesy of the Senator John Heinz History Center • 114John Trumbull • 116Library of Congress • 117©2008 Jupiterimages Corporation • 118National Park Service • 120United States Coast Guard • 122©2008 Jupiterimages Corporation • 124Henry R. Robinson •126William Wetmore Story • 128Adam sk (Wikimedia Commons) • 134Rembrandt Peale • 136Mathew Brady • 138John Trumbull • 140John Trumbull • 142www.wikipedia. com • 144Library of Congress • 146Mdiamante (Wikimedia Commons) • 148United States Army • 150John Trumbull • 156©2008 Jupiterimages Corporation • 158Courtesy Ronald Reagan Library • 160Samuel King • 162Department of Defense • 164Edmonston Studio • 166Henry S. Sadd • 168Photo provided by LeTourneau University www.letu.edu • 170National Park Service • 172Sarony & Major, 1846 • 174Thomas Gainsborough •176Emanuel Leutze; George A. Crofutt • 178George Bagby Matthews • 180Notman Photo Co., Boston, Mass • 184National Park Service, U.S. Department of the Interior • 186SrA Tana R. Hamilton • 188Richard SaltonstallGreenough • 190Chief Photographer's Mate (CPHOM) Robert F. Sargent • 194Library of Congress

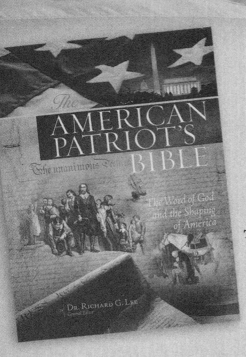